T0194746

The Shepherd Speaks . . . Do You Hear Him?

"Jesus demonstrated to His team that He wasn't a boss, but
a Shepherd that would lay down His life for the sheep."
Mike Breen 2016

Ron Warren

WESTBOW
PRESS®
A DIVISION OF THOMAS NELSON
& ZONDERVAN

WestBow Press books may be ordered through booksellers or by contacting:

WestBow Press
A Division of Thomas Nelson & Zondervan
1663 Liberty Drive
Bloomington, IN 47403
www.westbowpress.com
1 (866) 928-1240

ISBN: 978-1-9736-1519-4 (sc)
ISBN: 978-1-9736-1520-0 (hc)
ISBN: 978-1-9736-1518-7 (e)

Library of Congress Control Number: 2018900645

Print information available on the last page.

WestBow Press rev. date: 03/15/2018

CONTENTS

DEDICATION

This book is dedicated first to my lovely wife, co-worker and best friend, Jo, and secondly to my daughters Victoria and Charlotte, my sons-in-law, Phil and Andrew, and my three lovely grandchildren, Ione, Isla and Ava.

I give thanks for the millions of followers of the Shepherd around the world, who are living out their lives, fulfilling the call from heaven.

There are two individuals known to me that illustrate this last part.

The first is a close friend of Jo and me, who unfortunately must remain anonymous, and the country where she lives remain unidentified. She is around the same age as us, but when she sensed last year the call from the Shepherd to go and work at a special project, she released capital from her home in the UK and purchased a property in a country which today, is very unstable. We are very proud of her.

The second is a Gypsy Pastor in Romania, who must also remain anonymous. This amazing man's testimony is that during the communist era in his country, he was imprisoned and tortured. The communist regime's aim was to get him to renounce Jesus as the Son of God, and the way they did this was to take out his fingernails one at a time without pain relief. When he refused to renounce Jesus through this pain, the authorities then removed his teeth one by one without anaesthetic. He never did renounce his Saviour.

The Shepherd's people are serving in war torn countries, serving in food banks, advocating for the poor, supporting young people, working amongst the destitute, the list goes on and on and on. Not one of them seeking anything other than the knowledge that they are serving the living God.

People may not know who you are, you may not even be known in your home town or village, but one thing is for certain, the Shepherd knows who you are and what you are doing, and in His eyes, you are a wonderful success.

This book is also dedicated to the thousands of God's earthly shepherds who serve His people in small and large fellowships around the world, whether in cities, towns or villages. It doesn't matter if you serve in rich countries or in poor countries, the truth is without you, the church, which is the hope for the world, would struggle to fulfil the call on its life.

May the King of Heaven bless every one of you.

Introduction

THE SHEPHERD IS SPEAKING TO HIS CHURCH TODAY – ARE YOU LISTENING, CHURCH?

I never expected to write an essay let alone a book on this subject. I am not an established theologian, nor am I someone who seeks the limelight, but I am a practioner of the Gospel, that is Jesus of Nazareth, and for all my adult life with Him, I have sought, to the best of my ability, to follow the Shepherd's voice and do whatever He has asked me to do, for the sake of the gospel.

The following extract from the book, 'Hebrew Word Study: A Hebrew Teacher's Call to Silence', encapsulates for me, the very heart of this gospel that I love:

In silence my heart saw what my eyes could not see, my heart heard what my ears could not hear, and my heart spoke what my lips could not speak. In silence I was able to enter a special room in God's heart, a quiet room, a weeping room. In this room I found Jesus holding a heart in His hands, a heart which had been broken. He was weeping over that broken heart. He was feeling the heart's hurt and loneliness. He wept over that wounded heart longing so much to heal the wound that tore it apart, but the heart's owner would not seek His comfort. I saw Him pick up a heart that was cold and barren and watched His tear drops just roll off that heart. I could sense Him wishing that each tear would somehow penetrate that heart, but the

xi

heart's owner would not open it to Him to allow His tears to enter and soften his heart. As He picked up another broken heart I reached out to Him and touched His nail pierced hand and instantly I felt His sorrow and pain, the anguish felt by the heart's owner and I too wept. All three of us wept.

It was in this quiet, weeping room that I saw my own heart's desire. It was to not have a flourishing ministry, books published, or to even experience a healing of my body, it was only to seek and search for these heart's owners and let them know that there is a Saviour weeping for them, longing to enter their wounded heart to allow His tears, His nail pierced hands, to heal those wounds.

(Hebrew Word Study: A Hebrew Teacher's Call to Silence – Chaim Bentorah (16))

Right at the outset, I must declare that I am deeply in love with Jesus, and passionately sold out for the Kingdom of God. Everything I am and do, I hope, reflects this reality in my life.

I believe that when King Jesus came to the earth as a man through His mother Mary, He brought with Him the Kingdom of Heaven. I have believed this from the moment I started to follow the Shepherd. I also believe that we live in the 'now and not yet' of the Kingdom, and that until King Jesus returns to the earth in all His glory and majesty, there will continue to be battles and difficulties here in the earthly realm, but as some wise person said, "We are closer now to His coming than we have ever been". And as John says at the end of the book of Revelation, even so, '**Come, Lord Jesus**'. (Revelation 22:20 NIV)

In the preparation of this book, where I have quoted other authors, I have clearly identified where the quotes have come from. Most of the Bible verses used have been quoted from the New International Version.1 Where other versions have been used, that version has been identified and given full acknowledgement in the bibliography at the end of the book.

Just like most church leaders, I have attended numerous conferences over the years and listened to hundreds of sermons, and read hundreds of teaching notes on the Kingdom of God from leaders both inside and outside of the Vineyard Movement. During writing this book, I may inadvertently quote something that has stuck with me down the years, or taken from notes after listening to sermons from someone I can't remember and to which I cannot give a direct reference, so I ask for forgiveness in advance if this is the case.

Having declared all of that, I now come to the book itself.

I have had quite a few, what the Bible calls, visions in my life which have led my wife Jo and me on a wonderful journey of faith to many parts of this country and some wonderful places in God's world. On the other hand, I can't recall most of the dreams that I have had, especially those that border on the strange and weird.

Maybe it's my age!

In the last days, God says, I will pour out my Spirit on all people. Your sons and daughters will prophesy, your young men will see visions, *your old men will dream dreams.* (Acts 2:17 NIV) (Italics are mine)

At the very moment Jo and I decided that it was time to hand on the overall leadership of the Vineyard Church in Dartford to a younger couple; it seemed that my prayer life took on a different direction.

It had been our joy as a local gathering and part of the Body of Christ in Dartford, to pray for every other part of His Body in our town and to serve the people of the town well. Our mantra was always the verbal understanding of the picture of 'Vineyard Man' handed down to us through the Vineyard Movement – *'One foot in worship – One foot in compassion'.*

When we planted the Vineyard in Dartford, almost the first, what we might call prophetic word given to us was:

The Spirit of the Sovereign Lord is on me, because the Lord has anointed me to proclaim good news to the poor.

He has sent me to bind up the broken-hearted, to proclaim freedom for the captives and release from darkness for the prisoners. (Isaiah 61:1 NIV)

This vital word remained in the Vineyard Centre building in Dartford for a long time as a piece of remarkable artwork, reminding the ongoing church of the calling on its life.

My prayer life centred on these things, almost to the exclusion of all others. It may not have been a well-balanced prayer life, but it was certainly necessary for the work that we were called to do.

Now, most of my prayer life centres on, "Is there anything else you want me to do as we handover responsibility to others."

This is where the dream enters my life.

I had a dream that I remembered clearly, and as I woke, the dream remained with me, with more clarity and more detailed instructions for me to follow. I clearly remember the thought, that it seemed like the Shepherd wanted me in the dream to write a book, and the title of the book must be, "The Shepherd speaks, do you hear Him?" Over the following weeks, the titles of each chapter seemed to be revealed to me in further dreams, and so the outline was set.

To put this dream into perspective, the only other time I had anything like this was when I had a dream titled 'Village Aid', that I expand on in chapter 8, when I sensed the Shepherd showing me in a dream/vision the M25 London Ring Road on a map, and the Holy Spirit highlighting the major road junctions around the motorway. I was clearly able to see the North, East, South and West junctions, being the M1, the A2/M2, the M3 and the M4. (For anybody who doesn't know the road network in our country, these roads lead to the North, East, South and West.)

After praying through and asking the question, "What does this mean?" I sensed that I was being shown a prophetic picture of gates to a city and just how much God loves the city and that His blessings for the city will flow out through the gates to the surrounding countryside.

I didn't know what to do with this, and after good counsel from my church leader at the time, I waited patiently for the Shepherd to reveal to me anything He wanted me to do, if anything at all, with what He had shown me.

About a month later, whilst listening to Premier Christian Radio in my car, I heard an interview with a lady, who I had never heard of. With her husband, she was helping to lead a group of churches in the Watford area, north of London, and she told the interviewer about a picture that she felt might have come from Jesus. She then spoke about the picture she saw, which sounded identical to the one that I have described above. She went on to say that if anybody else had received the same picture, then please could they contact her, and she gave out her personal number for those people to use.

I was so excited that I phoned the minute I got out of my car, and this kind lady invited me to visit her on a certain date, when she said others would also be present.

It turned out that there were six of us who had the same dream/vision attending that meeting.

The reason for telling this story is that she told us at the time, she had to go on Premier Radio to speak out the dream/vision, as she felt that *'If she didn't do this, no one else would'*.

This book is written with the same sense that *'If I don't do this, nobody else will'*.

I have had the same confirmation that this lady had in as much as all the trusted friends I have spoken to about this project have confirmed that they believe it is something that I should do, which if ever finished, should bless the church. I am not sure if they thought I could even write a book, but I take their encouragement as a further instruction.

As I write I am reminded by the Shepherd of the following verse from the Book of Genesis,

He answered, "I heard you in the garden, and I was afraid because I was naked; so I hid." (Genesis 3:10 NIV)

My prayer is that if the book gets published, all who read it, will do so with open ears and an open heart, unlike Adam and Eve in their story, without being afraid of what the Shepherd may say and ask of you.

I trust that the following will help answer the question, 'Do you hear Him?' and I leave it in the safe hands of the Shepherd to do with it as He wills.

CHAPTER 1
MY STORY

Jo and I are the founding pastors of Gateway Vineyard Dartford, a family that we were highly privileged and honoured to serve until our retirement on Easter Sunday 2016.

As a boy growing up in the 1950s, I always knew that the world we lived in was larger and more frightening than it should be, and it was too much for a little boy to comprehend. I was a post-war baby living in South London, with the threat of a nuclear war in Europe at any time, and the world and the universe opening before me. I was an avid stamp collector throughout my young life, and this amazing hobby revealed to me, in a way that no teacher could, the vastness of the world and the countries that existed within it. Apart from the names of the nations and the names of their leaders, the stamps, through what was depicted on them, also taught me history, and the wonders that existed in the natural world. That stamp collection is now in the hands of my oldest granddaughter, and my hope is that she will learn as much about history, geography and the natural world as I have done.

At the same time as collecting stamps, I also collected an amazing set of cards from the tea makers, Brooke Bond Tea, which depicted the planets of our solar system. The book in which the cards were mounted, had a description of each planet, what each looked like and how far each was from Earth and the sun. The collection hinted at the larger universe, but without the stunning pictures that we now have through space

1

exploration and the Hubble Space Telescope, I think that hinting was about all they could do. (I would love to know where that book is now!)

Somehow, I knew something, but I didn't know what that something was!

To me, we all seemed so small and insignificant, and yet, the truth was that we were very important to those around us, and we were very much loved by the ones who loved us.

What a contradiction!

Throughout my teen years, the only thing that was important to me, was me. (not something to boast about) However, in my early twenties, I started on a spiritual journey, which included all the things that the Shepherd warns us against in the Bible: - tarot cards, mediums, star signs and much, much more. I didn't realise it at the time, but I believe now that the Shepherd was awakening something spiritual in me and I needed to follow it up. The problem was, I was going about it in the wrong way.

I couldn't understand it at the time, but somehow, I seemed to know that there was a huge god like universe and presumably, a huge god like figure holding everything together.

Today I can say that I know clearly that **'God is big. He is really, really big.'**

My true spiritual story, my life with the Shepherd, Jesus of Nazareth, starts in 1976, when I was twenty-nine. My wife Jo and I, had a little baby girl, we named Victoria. My mother, God bless her, insisted we should have her christened.

After an in-depth discussion with our local Anglican vicar, David Betts, we decided that we would do what my mum insisted.

A short time after the christening, Jo and I felt that we should honour a promise we made to David Betts, and attend the local Anglican church. This was the visible start of our journey together into faith.

After about a year of church going, both Jo and I felt that we needed to know more about this Jesus who was preached every week. There were various courses on faith in the church, and at the end of a short course on following Jesus, David prayed and then asked us to write down on a sheet of paper, the first thing that came into our mind. For me, this was the phrase "Teach Your Word".

That sheet of paper is still in the first Bible that I ever owned.

I had no understanding at the time, other than my mum's pestering words (very unusual for her), that this was the first time the Shepherd revealed Himself to me in a way that I recognized. Like the rest of that small seeking group in David's front room, it seemed to be scary, and for me it seemed utterly preposterous. But over the following weeks and months, I became more accustomed to hearing the voice of the Shepherd, as written down in the Bible.

As Jo and I became more involved in the local church life, both David and Irene, David's wife, threw us into service for Jesus. This meant that because of our infancy in the faith, we had to rely more and more on the still small voice of the Shepherd, which is of course, exactly why David and Irene did it. They fully understood the reality of Jesus' words, "I only do what the Father is doing."

Those years were an amazing time for us, as we were used all over the place relying on the voice of the Shepherd. For me, this culminated in attending, with other members of the church, a 'Signs and Wonders' conference at Wembley, where we encountered John Wimber and the Vineyard movement. I can still recall every part of that conference including the coach journeys both to and from Wembley, and everything in between. I was captivated.

Over the following years, Jo, our daughters Victoria and Charlotte and I, became more and more attuned to the voice of the Shepherd, and His call on our lives. When I was fifty-two, together with our very good friends Dave and Jill Adkin, the Shepherd called us to plant a Vineyard church in Dartford, our local town, with the help of Steve and Juliet Barber and the team at Southend Vineyard.

The Reason for this Book alongside the instructions from the Shepherd

As I said in the introduction, the beginning of considering and writing this book, is that of a practitioner of the Gospel, that is Jesus of Nazareth, and it relates to two things - one strategic and the other personal.

The first, and strategic reason, is comprised of the three questions invariably asked of me by new followers of Jesus: -

1) **What does it mean to hear from God?**
2) **What does hearing from God sound like?**
3) **How can I hear from God?**

The second and personal reason is prompted by the journey that I had with my dear friend, John Harris, who after suffering with cancer, is now at home with the King of Heaven. (John's earthly skills were logistics, and I can imagine him, even now, trying to help organise the heavenly following of his Shepherd!)

The Questions People Ask.

From being on a journey with people like David and Irene Betts, Bishop David Pytches, Barry Kissell, John Wimber, various New Wine leaders, Steve Barber, John and Eleanor Mumford, John and Debbie Wright (although many of them will never know how much they have impacted my spiritual life, and may not even agree with many of the things that I have written) and our friends in the Vineyard Movement in the United States. together with all the wonderful people that I have been in church with over the years, I have learned, deeply, that the Bible is God's inspired and relevant word for all time. Together with a vibrant prayer life, I have discovered down the years that reading God's word is the best and most reliable way to hear what He has to say to His followers about His creation, about the ways that He leads His followers, about the wonderful and complete restoration story of His Son, Jesus of Nazareth, and about the way to live a life full of hope, obedience, courage, joy and fulfilment.

When people ask, **'What does it look like to hear from God?'** I have consistently explained that for a clear and perfect understanding, they need to pray and read the Bible.

I encourage them to pray as if they were seated next to Jesus on His throne, and read the Bible first as a story. And then they should show how the passage they are reading fits into God's great salvation story. And finally, they should ask the Shepherd how what they are reading relates to them personally in today's world.

It is the Holy Spirit that brings the Shepherd's story to life as people read and pray. It is His presence in their lives that deepens their experience with Him. It's as if the words they are reading in the Bible jump off the page. And together with the Holy Spirit the reader begins to recognise that praying and reading the Bible are the clearest possible ways of hearing the voice of the Living God.

When people ask, **'How can I hear from God?'** I just tell them to approach prayer and the Bible with an open heart and without an agenda and just say, "Speak Lord, for Your servant is listening."

The Lord came and stood there, calling as at the other times, "Samuel! Samuel!" Then Samuel said, "Speak, for your servant is listening". (1 Samuel 3:10 NIV)

Finally, when they ask, **'What is the result of hearing God?'** I tell them that their changing lives and the impact they have on society is what it looks like.

The Shepherd has a plan for everyone created in His image. We must not be like Gideon, in the Old Testament. His approach was, "I can't possibly do what You, oh Lord, are asking me to do."

"Pardon me, my lord," Gideon replied, "but how can I save Israel? My clan is the weakest in Manasseh, and I am the least in my family." (Judges 6:15 NIV)

Father God knows us intimately, and He knows exactly what we need to enable us to live full and fruitful lives.

There are clear benefits to each of us if we listen to His voice and obey His instructions and there will be consequences if we ignore Him.

The journey with my friend John.

John was a man who talked about his conversations with Jesus as though they were both physically in the room together.

There are too many wonderful stories that John had to tell, but I have included two stand-out examples in his life with the Shepherd that clearly show what it is like living in the presence of the Shepherd. The first example was when we were both on a mission trip with other members of a team, to the north-west region of Bulgaria. We left the shores of Romania, where we were staying with a larger team, and when we landed on the Bulgarian side of the River Danube, we filled the two cars we drove over in with food purchased from a local store, (which, incidentally, almost emptied their stock) and together with the left-over cash from the money we took with us, set out to find a church where we could leave it all as a gift.

None of the team, including three Romanian friends who were with us, knew the area we were in, with only one of them speaking a smattering of Russian, and as the leader of the mission, I was beginning to panic as we needed to ensure that after delivering the food and money, we got back at the river crossing port to catch the last ferry back over the Danube into Romania, where we were all staying.

John spoke up. "I sense the church building we are looking for is in front of a 'Swiss Chalet' style building. Find that, and we will be at the right church".

If any readers have ever visited North West Bulgaria, you will know that most of the buildings in that area have the brutal architecture that is so often associated with former communist Eastern European states. Concrete tower block after concrete tower block.

We were a little sceptical to say the least.

After driving around for five to ten minutes, we arrived in a street close to the edge of the town centre, and there in the distance and to our surprise, we saw a 'Swiss Chalet' style building, and in front of it, a brand-new church building, which according to John is where we were supposed to be right from the start.

This was further confirmed to us when we walked in the building, as there was a mid-week worship service in progress, and to top it all, they were singing a well-known Vineyard song in their own language.

We had further confirmation that John had indeed heard the voice of the Shepherd, when after the service, the pastor, Valentin, told us that he had said to the congregation that before their meeting was over, they would see a miracle in front of their eyes. He didn't know in what form the miracle would take, but the food they needed, and the finances required for their outreach programme to the destitute villages around the town had just been delivered in their midst.

Pastor Valentin and his wife Vanya later told Jo and me that if their need and prayers had not been answered, then they were ready to walk away from their calling!

As an aside, it is true that those of us who follow the Shepherd, are very often the answer to other people's prayers.

There are benefits from hearing and responding to the voice of the Shepherd and there are consequences from not doing so, not just for us but for others too.

On our way back to the ferry, I asked John, "Tell me again how you were so certain that the 'Swiss Chalet' style building was the answer to our considerable problem?"

John's answer was simple and to the point – "I believe that Jesus showed me a picture of the building".

The second example starts from when John first heard that he had cancer. John told me that he sensed Father God reveal to him that the surgery and subsequent medication would be painful and difficult, but he would get through it. The truth is that it was certainly painful for John, but as he sensed, he did get through it.

John's second experience of cancer was completely different. On a hospital visit, John told me that this time he sensed that Father God was revealing to him that it will be much more difficult, but that He would be close to him, and the outcome this time would be complete healing, and that would be the time when they would meet face to face in glory".

I tell my dear friend's two stories not just for information, but also to reveal how a relationship with the true Shepherd can fundamentally change the way we live our lives here on the earth.

The security that John had in the presence of the Shepherd is the same security that you and I can have today.

There can be clear benefits if we hear and obey the voice of the Shepherd, and there could be dire consequences if we ignore Him.

Question:

Do these stories excite you, and is your heart longing for such a relationship with the Shepherd, the King of Heaven?

If the answer is yes, then turn your thoughts to Heaven and ask the Shepherd to guide you. I would encourage you to write down every thought that enters your head together with any texts in the bible that the Shepherd may lead you to.

CHAPTER 2
THE SHEPHERD IN THE OLD TESTAMENT

I have noticed through my own walk and life lived with the Shepherd, that there have been times of clearly hearing His voice and times when I totally ignored His words in my ear. There just seem to be so many voices seeking to impact my life! Those other voices include everything you could think of, ranging from deep voices within my own being, through to lies spoken over me by the enemy of all mankind, and everything else in between.

For the past fifteen years or so, I have noticed the same reality in the lives of the followers of Jesus in the Vineyard Church in Dartford, who have graciously allowed Jo and I to pastor them. It doesn't seem to matter whether they have been full of faith for most of their lives, or they have just come to faith. Just like me, the voices seem to speak louder and louder.

We can and should make a choice between all the competing voices. We are either going to listen to the loving creator of all things, or we are going to listen to lies. There are clearly rewards for listening to His voice and consequences for ignoring Him.

To understand more fully the analogy of the Shepherd and the sheep, we need to first interrogate the Old Testament and see what it reveals about the matter.

Before we get into that, the first thing we must do, prior to delving into this chapter, is look at the ways God spoke to His people when either enjoying their company or seeking to direct them in all His ways.

After speaking all things into existence, we find Father God conversing with His first human creation, Adam, in a way that you and I would speak to each other.

15 The Lord God took the man and put him in the Garden of Eden to work it and take care of it. 16 And the Lord God commanded the man, "You are free to eat from any tree in the garden; 17 but you must not eat from the tree of the knowledge of good and evil, for when you eat from it you will certainly die."

18 The Lord God said, "It is not good for the man to be alone. I will make a helper suitable for him."

19 Now the Lord God had formed out of the ground all the wild animals and all the birds in the sky. He brought them to the man to see what he would name them; and whatever the man called each living creature, that was its name. 20 So the man gave names to all the livestock, the birds in the sky and all the wild animals. But for Adam no suitable helper was found. 21 So the Lord God caused the man to fall into a deep sleep; and while he was sleeping, he took one of the man's ribs and then closed up the place with flesh. 22 Then the Lord God made a woman from the rib he had taken out of the man, and he brought her to the man.
(Genesis 2:15-22 NIV)

Can you imagine what that must have felt like? Adam's only point of reference at that time was his creator, Father God. There was no one else in all of creation that he could talk with. (In my quieter times, I often think about the language they would have used? I guess this might just be my crazy way of thinking, or are there others out there with the same thoughts?)

The next time we hear God speak is after Adam and Eve did their thing eating the forbidden fruit in the garden.

8 Then the man and his wife heard the sound of the Lord God as he was walking in the garden in the cool of the day, and they hid from the Lord God among the trees of the garden. 9 But the Lord God called to the man, "Where are you?"

10 He answered, "I heard you in the garden, and I was afraid because I was naked; so I hid."

11 And he said, "Who told you that you were naked? Have you eaten from the tree that I commanded you not to eat from?"

12 The man said, "The woman you put here with me—she gave me some fruit from the tree, and I ate it."

13 Then the Lord God said to the woman, "What is this you have done?" The woman said, "The serpent deceived me, and I ate." (Genesis 3:8-13 NIV)

We still see direct one to one conversations between Father God and His created people. My own belief is that this type of intimacy and interaction was finally restored to all mankind at the crucifixion of Jesus the Messiah, when the curtain was torn from top to bottom.

The next important moments when God speaks directly to His people, is when we read the stories of Abraham and Moses.

The Old Testament confirms these conversations had happened, as recorded in the following two verses:

When he had finished speaking with Abraham, God went up from him.
(Genesis 17:22 NIV)

When the Lord finished speaking to Moses on Mount Sinai, he gave him the two tablets of the covenant law, the tablets of stone inscribed by the finger of God.
(Exodus 31:18 NIV)

In Deuteronomy chapters 4 and 5, we can see that many others are recorded to have heard the thunderous voice of God out of the fire on the mountain, and it seems quite clear to me that if this type of thing continued to happen, not many of them expected to hear the voice of God and live.

It is fascinating to me that when we look at the instructions that God gives to Moses about Aaron and his role as His First High Priest, that God seemed to know that it was very difficult for man to stand in His presence and live. God's graciousness covers every eventuality. There would be no misunderstanding for those waiting outside of the Holy of Holies – If the bells on the bottom of his tunic rang out, the High Priest had been in the presence of the Living God and lived.

34 The gold bells and the pomegranates are to alternate around the hem of the robe. 35 Aaron must wear it when he ministers. The sound of the bells will be heard when he enters the Holy Place before the Lord and when he comes out, so that he will not die.
(Exodus 28:34-35 NIV)

With this interesting piece of instruction, I can't help but think that God has covered every eventuality throughout the universe and for all time.

If we read on, we can hear God speaking with Cain, and still later, with Noah. Once you get to the end of Exodus, you would have heard God talking to people by means of dreams, through angels, and from a burning bush. These words undergird the first part of the statement with which the letter to the Hebrews begins: **In the past God spoke to our ancestors through the prophets at many times and in various ways.** (Hebrews 1:1 NIV)

I have always thought that the following was, and still is a great question. "How did God speak to His prophets?"

From the passages of scripture, it seems clear to me that God spoke to each of His prophets directly through visions and dreams. They saw them in depth and with great clarity, and on waking up from their sleep, recorded exactly what they saw and heard.

For a great example of this, I invite you to read what Isaiah wrote when he woke up and remembered a dream from God:

1 In the year that King Uzziah died, I saw the Lord, high and exalted, seated on a throne; and the train of his robe filled the temple. 2 Above him were seraphim, each with six wings: With two wings they covered their faces, with two they covered their feet, and with two they were flying. 3 And they were calling to one another:

"Holy, holy, holy is the Lord Almighty;
the whole earth is full of his glory."
(Isaiah 6:1-3 NIV)

Once awake, he remembers each part of the dream with clear thought, and each word is carefully written down with care for all who were to follow him.

You and I surely benefit today from Isaiah's obedience?

By studying the Old Testament, you will find in the lives of prophet after prophet, that the way God communicates between Himself and His prophets always seems to bear the same hallmark. As an example, just look at Daniel:

In the first year of Belshazzar king of Babylon, Daniel had a dream, and visions passed through his mind as he was lying in bed. He wrote down the substance of his dream. (Daniel 7:1 NIV)

He writes a little further on:

1 In the third year of King Belshazzar's reign, I, Daniel, had a vision, after the one that had already appeared to me. 2 In my vision I saw myself in the citadel of Susa in the province of Elam; in the vision I was beside the Ulai Canal. (Daniel 8:1-2 NIV)

It seems that regardless of who the prophet was, and regardless of the message revealed, God spoke to His prophets through a one-off visitation in visions and dreams' in which they clearly heard the voice of God, saw how it fitted into God's unfolding plan, then faithfully wrote down each detailed word so that it would be recorded for all time.

Back to the question, how did God speak to His prophets?

He spoke words of love, whether it be for approval, correction or direction. (As an aside, I believe the Bible teaches us that if we receive a prophetic word from heaven for someone or some situation they find themselves in, then it must always be delivered in love and build-up that person for their continued walk with the Shepherd. It should be the same for us when a brother or sister speaks into our lives.)

Hopefully you can see from the above notes, and from reading the Bible, that it was not normal for most of mankind to get messages directly from God. The normal way of things then and therefore now, was that mankind got indirect revelation from those that God had chosen. The prophets themselves did not get a direct revelation concerning anything that was on their mind at the time, or at the specific moment of time when they thought they should get it. It wasn't something that man could demand or insist upon. It wasn't then, and it isn't now.

As I have written in depth elsewhere, beginning with the Law of Moses, the Written Word of God is the normal way to receive revelation. It is also the safest.

When God did speak, it had to be written down, and that written word was needed as the resource for daily guidance in most people's lives throughout history.

Moses wrote down the law that was revealed to him and warned the people of Israel to:

58 If you do not carefully follow all the words of this law, which are written in this book, and do not revere this glorious and awesome name—the Lord your God— 59 the Lord will send fearful plagues on you and your descendants, harsh and prolonged disasters, and severe and lingering illnesses. (Deuteronomy 28:58-59 NIV)

Joshua, who also received revelations from God, was told:

Keep this Book of the Law always on your lips; meditate on it day and night, so that you may be careful to do everything written in it. Then you will be prosperous and successful. (Joshua 1:8 NIV)

Hopefully you will see that as we go on with our subject, that God's words to us today, are revealed through His written word, and that He is dealing with us just as He has dealt with most people throughout history. We must test everything we hear and read, against the revealed word of God in the Bible.

So, on with the rest of this book.

It seems clear that there is a distinct difference between people who are without a shepherd and those who seek to live their lives under the guidance, gaze and voice of the Shepherd.

There are two important words that occur again and again in scripture, and these are:

'Shepherd' – 'Poimen'

Strongs #4166

'A herdsman, shepherd, one who tends, leads, cherishes, feeds, and protects a flock'.

'Feed' – 'Ra'ah'

Strongs #7462

'To shepherd, feed, tend, to pasture, to cause one's herd or flock to graze'.

These two words clearly talk about protection, feeding, safety and leading. They convey the sense that all will be well, and all things will be well.

Let's look first at the positive side of the story of God as a Shepherd as revealed by the Old Testament writers Moses, David, Asaph, Isaiah and Ezekiel.

In Genesis 48:15, Moses records the following: **The God who has been my shepherd all my life.** (NIV)

This is Jacob speaking in his old age, where he reflects on his God and then uses his own history with the Shepherd, during his blessing of Joseph's two sons, Manasseh and Ephraim.

In Genesis 49:24, Moses now speaks of **The Shepherd, the Rock of Israel.** (NIV)

In Colin Urquhart's 'The Truth version of the Bible', 2 he helpfully puts it like this – **His arms remained strong because the hands of the mighty God of Jacob were upon him. He is The Shepherd, the Rock of Israel, and your father's God who helps you.**

This speech comes during Jacob's last words to his sons, the twelve tribes of Israel, when he uses the titles 'The Shepherd' and the 'Rock of Israel'.

Such titles as these being rare in the Old Testament, we should none the less, not minimise the importance of the words.

In Psalm 23:1, David cries out at the beginning of his song, **The Lord is my Shepherd, I shall not want.** (NIV)

This is an amazing reflection from an earthly shepherd, who himself knows how a shepherd acts and what he needs to do if he is going to work hard to protect his flock.

David the shepherd looks to God's provision from the beginning of time to the fulfilment of all things with the coming of the True Shepherd, King Jesus.

With the Shepherd in His rightful place, David knows that all his needs will be met, even in the valley of the shadow of death, the last deadly frontier for all mankind.

At this point, I am reminded of two of the closest men I have known, one of whom spoke directly to me just before dying and the other speaking in my presence just before he passed on.

The first was my very dear friend, Terry Simpson, who just hours before he passed on, lovingly took my head in his hands, and with my tears pouring over him, he said, "It is OK. Everything we believe is real."

The second was my wonderful dad, who just before passing on, awoke from a 'coma like' existence, leaned up from his pillow, and said to a person unseen by me at the foot of his bed, "What should I do then?" My dad smiled, laid back down, and passed on that night.

Terry was a longstanding follower of Jesus, and to the best of my knowledge, my dad, up to the point that I have talked about, had never really considered Jesus in any serious way.

I have never been more convinced that:

"Even though I walk
through the darkest valley,
I will fear no evil,
for you are with me;
your rod and your staff,
they comfort me".
(Psalm 23:4 NIV)

In Psalm 28:9 David says about the Lord being the people's strength, that He will **be their Shepherd and carry them forever.** (NIV)

Here, David again talks about Yahweh as a Shepherd, being the people's saving refuge together with overseeing their shelter. Wouldn't you want to be in that reality?

In Psalm 80:1, a Psalm of Asaph, the psalmist says, **Hear us, o Shepherd of Israel.** (NIV)

This is a declaration, a song directly sung to the Shepherd of Israel, to the one who leads Joseph like a flock. The psalmist continues to ask the Shepherd to 'shine forth' before Ephraim, Benjamin and Manasseh, the three tribes who followed next to the Ark when Israel was on the move. (Numbers 2:17-24)

In Isaiah 40:11, the prophet says that **He tends His flock like a shepherd.** (NIV)

'Tend' used here is another word for 'feed' (Ra'ah), which is to do with tending and caring for one's animals, particularly by providing them with good pasture.

Isaiah here is talking about a God who cares deeply for His people, like a shepherd who will do anything to protect his flock at all cost.

The great theologian, and the one on whose shoulders I sit in these matters, Matthew Henry in his Commentary on the whole Bible (3), puts verse 11 like this: -

"The same God that rules with a strong hand of a Prince leads and feeds with the kind hand of a shepherd." He goes on to say, "He will gather them in when they wander, gather them up when they fall, gather them together when they are dispersed, and gather them home to Himself at last; and all this with His own arms, out of which none shall be able to pluck them".

What an amazing description of a loving Father.

Lastly in this section, we have the prophet Ezekiel speaking, about 'God the true Shepherd'.

11'For this is what the Sovereign Lord says: I myself will search for my sheep and look after them. 12 As a shepherd looks after his scattered flock when he is with them, so will I look after my sheep. I will rescue them from all the places where they were scattered on a day of clouds and darkness. 13 I will bring them out from the nations and gather them from the countries, and I will bring them into their own land. I will pasture them on the mountains of Israel, in the ravines and in all the settlements in the land. 14 I will tend them in a good pasture, and the mountain heights of Israel will be their grazing land. There they will lie down in good grazing land, and there they will feed in a rich pasture on the mountains of Israel. 15 I myself will tend my sheep and have them lie down, declares the Sovereign Lord. 16 I will search for the lost and bring back the strays. I will bind up the injured and strengthen the weak, but the sleek and the strong I will destroy. I will shepherd the flock with justice'.
(Ezekiel 34:11-16 NIV)

You are my sheep, the sheep of my pasture, and I am your God, declares the Sovereign Lord. (Ezekiel 34:31 NIV)

This is Ezekiel the prophet revealing the actions that the true Shepherd will undertake, which are in direct contrast to those of the false shepherds of the day. (These, I believe, are still around today in God's church, telling people that they can do it better themselves, that by better understanding they can live more fulfilled lives, that by giving more money they can be more blessed, etc.)

These verses foretell Jesus, the good Shepherd.

v.11 "I Myself will search for my sheep."

v.12 "I will look after my sheep."

v.13 "I will bring them out."

v.13 "I will pasture them."

v.14 "I will tend them."

v.15 "I will tend my sheep."

v.15 "I will have them lie down."

v.16 "I will search for the lost."

v.16 "I will... bring back the strays."

v.16 "I will... bind up the injured...."

V.16 "I will... strengthen the weak..."

(Ezekiel 34:11-16 NIV)

(Compare this list with that in John 10 verses 2-16, unpacked later in chapter 5)

With these words, the true Shepherd shows that He will do the very things which His earthly shepherds are supposed to do and haven't done too well.

Not only does the true Shepherd show the difference between how He works and how different that is to the way the false shepherds act, but if you read further in verses 17-19, He also speaks to the individual members of His flock.

It is clear from this passage that the 'sheep' themselves are not 'off the hook', just because their earthly shepherds were bad.

Just as God holds the shepherds accountable for how they treat the people entrusted to them, He also holds each member of the flock accountable for how they treat each other.

Among the flock itself would be those who would have been helping to destroy the flock. These may have been the leaders and elders of their day, or they could just be people seeking to enrich their lifestyle, or indeed they may have been people seeking to destroy the fellowship. Who they were is not clear, but one thing is for certain, they weren't helping. They would get to drink the clear fresh water and then muddy the stream for those coming behind them. Their selfishness would have been obvious to all those around them, as at the same time, it would have been harmful to those who came next to drink.

We must not confuse this passage with the separation of the sheep and goats that Jesus talks about in Matthew 25:31-46. Here Ezekiel is contrasting the fat, wealthy and strong, with the hungry, poor and the weak.

As an aside, maybe today this continues to happen when it seems that the rich around the world are getting richer and the poor are getting poorer? It seems clear to me from the passage that there is never a situation in our lives where we are not accountable for the depth and breadth of our lives to each other.

THAT IS THE POSITIVE SIDE.

THE NEGATIVE SIDE.

Numbers 27:17. This is Moses being told that Joshua was to be the next leader of Israel. God says to Moses tell him **to go out and come in before them, one who will lead them out and bring them in, so the Lord's people will not be like sheep without a shepherd.** (NIV)

1 Kings 22:17 is a prophetic word picture from Micaiah, **I saw all Israel scattered on the hills like sheep without a shepherd.** (NIV)

2 Chronicles 18:16 has the same account as written in 1 Kings 22:17. (When this happens in the Bible, maybe we should take special note.)

Isaiah 13:14 says, **Like sheep without a shepherd.** *(NIV)*

Ezekiel 34:5 & 8. Here is the opposite of what we saw in verses 11-31.

v.5 They were scattered because there was no shepherd. (NIV)

v.8 Because my flock lacks a shepherd. (NIV)

To the leaders of God's people of that day, leadership wasn't about service but power. They didn't lead to help and protect, but to boost their own power. This truth reveals itself in Jesus' day, when the Sanhedrin go to work on Him! Unfortunately, because we are only human, it can still be found today throughout the world with some leaders seeking to consolidate power rather than serving, as Jesus instructed us to do. There is a further problem that could arise if leadership is not under authority, and that is abuse.

Therefore, in the Vineyard church worldwide, as with many other church movements, leaders who are under authority, do not sit at the pinnacle of all things – they sit at the bottom serving as best they can, to help and protect the people that God has called on the journey with them. John Mumford would say that the worldly pyramid of leadership structures must be turned upside down in God's church, with the leaders serving the followers of Jesus, emulating the 'washing of feet' example that Jesus showed His followers after the last supper. Most of you who are followers of Jesus today are following Him because of how leaders, or if you like, earthly shepherds, have sought to lead you in this journey that we are all on together.

The results of God's so-called shepherds of His flock were catastrophic. The people God loved, whom He redeemed from Egypt were starved, scattered, and torn to pieces. Our prayer must be that it would not happen again in our day.

Finally, we see in Zechariah 10:2 a statement about the outcome of those who follow, worship and bow down to idols.

Diviners see visions that lie;
they tell dreams that are false,
they give comfort in vain.
Therefore, the people wander like sheep. (NIV)

The idols speak to humans deceitfully, and those people are oppressed for lack of a shepherd.

Through the prophet Zechariah, God contrasts the difference between His ways and the ways of the enemies of His people.

The idols or enemies, devour, lie, and tell false dreams and they comfort in vain. How many people's lives have been shattered because of lies and false dreams?

This way, God says, leads to people wandering around like sheep, getting into difficulty and trouble, becoming hungry and thirsty, all as if there were no shepherd.

In a world where truth, justice and trust seem to have disappeared from public life, and where peace for many millions of people is a 'pipe-dream', one could argue very strongly that the enemy of all mankind has sway everywhere!

This is not the truth, and it needs to be spoken out as loudly as possible. There is an absolute truth, and it underlies everything that exists, and it is available to all people, everywhere, for free.

There is no secret to freedom – freedom is only found in and through the Messiah, Jesus of Nazareth.

The church of Christ must energise itself through the power of the Holy Spirit, move outside of its walls of fear, and declare unashamedly that Jesus is Lord. We can't do it in our own strength, or with our own ideas, no matter how clever they may seem. Energising must come through waiting on the Lord, discovering His thumbprint for individual fellowships and then doing whatever He tells us to do.

What is the worst that could happen to us?

With the True Shepherd, there is truth, justice, freedom, trust, life, hope and love.

Questions:

1) Do you live your life as though you are in charge? Are you seeking out other ways of finding meaning for your life or would you prefer someone show you where to find safety and live in a place where there is good pasture, which would include safety, peace of mind and a settled life?

2) If the answer is yes to the third part of the question, what do you think that might look like and how do you think you could test it?

CHAPTER 3
THE SHEPHERD IN THE NEW TESTAMENT

It is not surprising to me that the first people – other than Mary and Joseph, the parents of Jesus – who come into the presence of 'The Lamb who would take away the sins of the world', were earthly shepherds. Why would it be any different with a Living God who knows exactly the best ways to reveal His Son? At His direction, the heavenly realm directed them where to go and what to do, which was, if you like, a picture of what was to come when the 'True Shepherd' would call all mankind unto Himself.

Look at the response of the shepherds.

8 And there were shepherds living out in the fields nearby, keeping watch over their flocks at night. 9 An angel of the Lord appeared to them, and the glory of the Lord shone around them, and they were terrified. 10 But the angel said to them, 'Do not be afraid. I bring you good news that will cause great joy for all the people. 11 Today in the town of David a Saviour has been born to you; he is the Messiah, the Lord. 12 This will be a sign to you: you will find a baby wrapped in cloths and lying in a manger.'

13 Suddenly a great company of the heavenly host appeared with the angel, praising God and saying,

14 'Glory to God in the highest heaven,

and on earth peace to those on whom his favour rests.'

15 When the angels had left them and gone into heaven, the shepherds said to one another, 'Let's go to Bethlehem and see this thing that has happened, which the Lord has told us about.'

16 So they hurried off and found Mary and Joseph, and the baby, who was lying in the manger. 17 When they had seen him, they spread the word concerning what had been told them about this child, 18 and all who heard it were amazed at what the shepherds said to them. 19 But Mary treasured up all these things and pondered them in her heart. 20 The shepherds returned, glorifying and praising God for all the things they had heard and seen, which were just as they had been told. (Luke 2:8-20 NIV)

They just couldn't seem to help themselves. They were overjoyed and full of praise for what and who they had seen. I don't know about you, but I would be more than happy with just one angel turning up to do this for me!

It is amazing to think that from His very beginnings as a man here on the earth, the Good Shepherd sent by His Heavenly Father, is greeted by earthly shepherds who know exactly how a shepherd should behave regarding his sheep.

I love the fact that Jesus' mother, Mary, **treasured up all these things and pondered them in her heart.** The memory of them, together with all that happened when the Magi, or as described elsewhere, the Wise Men from the East, came and left their gifts for her son, must have been a constant reminder and help to Mary as, along with Joseph, she raised Jesus into adulthood.

It would be helpful now to look at the timescale of the Shepherd, as He ministered here on the earth. The last three years of His earthly life are covered well in scripture, and it would be impossible to cover every recorded situation where He ministered in one chapter of one book. I have therefore chosen two different situations in that period, which hopefully, can help us understand what the Shepherd was doing.

The first story relates to a time when there were Pharisees, teachers of the Law, tax collectors and sinners (Perhaps they should all just be called sinners!) gathering around Jesus.

1 Now the tax collectors and sinners were all gathering around to hear Jesus. 2 But the Pharisees and the teachers of the law muttered, 'This man welcomes sinners, and eats with them.'

3 Then Jesus told them this parable: 4 'Suppose one of you has a hundred sheep and loses one of them. Doesn't he leave the ninety-nine in the open country and go after the lost sheep until he finds it? 5 And when he finds it, he joyfully puts it on his shoulders 6 and goes home. Then he calls his friends and neighbours together and says, "Rejoice with me; I have found my lost sheep." 7 I tell you that in the same way there will be more rejoicing in heaven over one sinner who repents than over ninety-nine righteous people who do not need to repent. (Luke 15:3-7 NIV)

The Shepherd is clearly revealing in this story His purpose here on the earth, and why He came, albeit in parable form, and it left those who were with Him, those who had ears to hear, in no doubt that the Shepherd has come, and He would 'seek and save the lost'.

Notice how the shepherd does three things for His sheep:

First, he searches.

Can you see how the shepherd is anxious to recover the lost sheep — He leaves the ninety-nine immediately to go after the one who is lost. Can you also see that the shepherd doesn't give up until the sheep is found — He goes after the sheep until he finds it. Now we see a very welcoming approach from the shepherd, he isn't angry at the sheep for getting lost, after all, it is its nature to wander off — He is joyful when he finds his sheep.

This echoes the Shepherd when He came out of heaven to save all that has been made since the beginning of time, that is all of everything, and all of mankind living in the past and those yet to come, from the power of sin and destruction. She will give birth to a son, and you are to give him the name Jesus, because he will save his people from their sins. (Matthew 1:21 NIV) For the Son of Man came to seek and to save the lost. (Luke 19:10 NIV)

Secondly, he finds.

When the shepherd finds the lost sheep, you can see that he carries all its weight. The sheep is carried on his shoulders. Not only does he carry the weight, the shepherd also keeps the sheep safe. The sheep are safe and held firmly in his grip. (I am so reminded of the footsteps in the sand poem!)

In the same way as the earthly shepherd, Jesus carries the weight of sin for each of us. **Come to me, all you who are weary and burdened, and I will give you rest.** (Matthew 11:28 NIV) He also holds our salvation safe and secure. **I give them eternal life, and they shall never perish; no one will snatch them out of my hand.** (John 10:28 NIV)

Thirdly, he brings the sheep home.

Look and see how the shepherd brings the sheep all the way home and then shares his joy of finding the sheep with his friends. The sheep is home, safe and sound. He is compelled to tell his friends the wonderful news so that they can share in it.

Here again is the Good News of the gospel.

When a person comes to Jesus, **I tell you that in the same way there will be more rejoicing in heaven over one sinner who repents than over ninety-nine righteous people who do not need to repent.** (Luke

15:7 NIV) The promise of the Good News is that Jesus doesn't leave us on our own, He leads us to heaven. 2 **My Father's house has many rooms; if that were not so, would I have told you that I am going there to prepare a place for you? 3. And if I go and prepare a place for you, I will come back and take you to be with me that you also may be where I am.** (John 14:2-3 NIV)

It would probably have been a lot easier for us to understand this parable, if we had lived in the first century A.D. If we lived in the country villages, and not the cities, our resources and overall welfare would have been tied up with farming, sheep and goats and fishing. Imagine what it would have been like if your sheep or goat had got lost? No offspring to slaughter and eat, no milk or cheese to provide for your family, and perhaps worst of all, no animal to offer as a sacrifice to Yahweh. It would be catastrophic. Our friends would be anxious for us, and we would be distraught. Oh, for the shepherd to find our lost one!

If we are distraught at a lost sheep or goat, just think how our heavenly Father feels, when He sees any one of us, made in His image, lost?

If any of you feels like this with your family, friends and work colleagues, there is no better encouragement for you to tell them about the Shepherd, than this parable.

The second story, is the well-known one about Jesus and Zacchaeus the tax collector.

1 **Jesus entered Jericho and was passing through. 2 A man was there by the name of Zacchaeus; he was a chief tax collector and was wealthy. 3 He wanted to see who Jesus was, but because he was short he could not see over the crowd. 4 So he ran ahead and climbed a sycamore-fig tree to see him, since Jesus was coming that way.**

5 **When Jesus reached the spot, he looked up and said to him, 'Zacchaeus, come down immediately. I must stay at your house today.' 6 So he came down at once and welcomed him gladly.**

7 All the people saw this and began to mutter, 'He has gone to be the guest of a sinner.'

8 But Zacchaeus stood up and said to the Lord, 'Look, Lord! Here and now I give half of my possessions to the poor, and if I have cheated anybody out of anything, I will pay back four times the amount.'

9 Jesus said to him, 'Today salvation has come to this house, because this man, too, is a son of Abraham. 10 For the Son of Man came to seek and to save the lost.' (Luke 19:1-10 NIV)

We could spend pages and pages on the man Zacchaeus, and it would benefit us to do it, but this book is about the Shepherd, and that is where we must concentrate our gaze.

He is the seeking saviour of all mankind, and this story reveals to us the way the Good Shepherd works.

First, Jesus came to Zacchaeus. Even though He knew everything there was to know about him, both good and bad, He still loved him and had compassion on him, and then finally, He called him.

This is the way He always works. Have you not seen it yet?

Firstly, the Shepherd comes to each one of us and offers life through Himself. There is no other way. He knows us better than we do ourselves, and if He didn't show us our need, we would never be able to see it in ourselves. We wouldn't be able to, or even have the desire to come to Jesus, unless He came to us first.

Secondly, the Shepherd knows everything there is to know about us, and even with that knowledge, He still loves us and would save us by His grace if we would only come to Him and receive Him.

Thirdly, the Shepherd calls us. Here is the echo of the shepherd calling for the lost sheep. Who was this man, Zacchaeus, that Jesus would stop on the road to speak to? He was a sinner, yet the Shepherd loved him, just like He loves you and me.

What was this call like?

Firstly, it was an urgent call. **"Zacchaeus, come down immediately."** Can you hear the echoes of it?

And secondly, it was an unmistakable call. Jesus was looking for more than just a place to visit for the day.

Jesus was, and still is today, looking for one thing, and one thing only, He is after your heart. **"I must stay at your house today."**

When reading this passage, do you see what is in front of your eyes?

In the story, there is a seeking sinner, Zacchaeus, and there is a seeking shepherd, Jesus. Look at it this way. If there was a seeking sinner, you, there certainly is a seeking shepherd, Jesus.

The Shepherd is always at work, seeking the lost, and I beg you to be prepared, as He might come to you at any unexpected moment in time. (I recall again my wonderful dad!)

Finally, in this story we see the mercy of Jesus, and we see the mission of Jesus.

The Mercy of Jesus – Jesus said to him, 'Today salvation has come to this house, because this man, too, is a son of Abraham'. (verse 9) Jesus takes Zacchaeus, a corrupt tax collector, and in a second, saves him forever.

If you do not know the saving grace of God for yourself, the Shepherd can reveal it to you, and do the same for you today as He did for Zacchaeus over two thousand years ago.

The Mission of Jesus – 'For the Son of Man came to seek and to save the lost'. (verse 10) In this final part of the story, Jesus reminds us that He came out of heaven to save sinners, by living an earthly life as a man, dying on a cross in our place and being fully resurrected on the third day. This mission that Jesus' Father sent Him for, has never stopped, and will not stop until the wonderful day when He will return in all His glory.

There are so many amazing stories like this in the books of Matthew, Mark, Luke and John, in the New Testament, and I encourage you to look at them in a way that helps you understand more fully, the mercy and mission of the Shepherd. It is the most revealing way that the Shepherd speaks today and for all time, and if you do look, you will hear the call of the Shepherd, and when you do, just as Mary instructed, do what He tells you to do.

There are benefits from hearing and responding to the voice of the Shepherd and there are consequences from not doing so.

Questions:

1) *Do you feel lost? If so, know that the Shepherd is searching for you, and that He will find you. When He does, it is then up to you. Would you choose to go your own way, or would you choose to let the Shepherd take you home?*

2) *Are you a seeker? If so, know that the Shepherd is also seeking – He is seeking you right now. How do you think you would respond if He made Himself known to you?*

CHAPTER 4
THE SHEPHERD AND CREATION

The whole of Creation as a subject, is far too vast for this book, and therefore, I can only talk about where we are right now. Having said that, as it takes the light from the Sun an average of 8 minutes and 20 seconds to travel from the Sun to the Earth, I am not even sure that knowing where we are right now, is a correct statement? It wasn't that long ago, about 2,400 years, that the people up until that time, described the world as a dome or an upturned bowl. It wasn't until people sailed the seas that they finally knew for sure that the world, is indeed, round. (Some people today still argue that the world is flat!)

The ground feels firm and solid beneath our feet, which of course it is. We know that the Earth is rotating, turning once on its axis every day. Fortunately for us, gravity keeps us firmly attached to the planet, and because of momentum, we don't even feel the movement – the same way we might not feel the speed of a car we are in going down the highway, or sitting in a plane flying across the sky. I think that probably skydiving is the only real way of experiencing speed, but unlike my younger daughter, I have no intention of experiencing it for myself!

If we look at a spot on the surface of the Earth, perhaps where we are standing or sitting, are we aware that it is moving at about 1675 km/h or 460 meters/second? That's roughly 1,000 miles/hour. Just think for a second!!! – that second has just moved us almost half a kilometre through space, and we didn't even feel it.

If we can't even experience this, how is it possible to get our minds around the complexities of creation?

Let us try…

A beautiful evening was arranging its finery over the bay and the warm stone of the village streets. He could see more colours than he could even hope to name, delicate shades of pink and blue, tones that slipped from gold to pale ochre and back again even as he watched, a dozen varieties of silver. Beauty that only God could create. Beauty beyond man's comprehension.

What do you think? These are evocative words written about God's creation, by the author Kevin Doherty, in his novel, 'Villa Normandie' (13)

Let us look at what the Bible says about **all things**?

The beginning of all things

1-2

First this: God created the Heavens and Earth—all you see; all you don't see. Earth was a soup of nothingness, a bottomless emptiness, an inky blackness. God's Spirit brooded like a bird above the watery abyss.

3-5

God spoke: "Light!" And light appeared. God saw that light was good and separated light from dark. God named the light Day, he named the dark Night. It was evening, it was morning— *Day One.*

6-8

God spoke: "Sky! In the middle of the waters; separate water from water!" God made sky. He separated the water under sky from the water above sky. And there it was: he named sky the Heavens; It was evening, it was morning— *Day Two.*

9-10

God spoke: "Separate! Water-Beneath-Heaven, gather into one place; Land, appear!" And there it was. God named the land Earth. He named the pooled water Ocean. God saw that it was good.

11-13

God spoke: "Earth, green up! Grow all varieties of seed-bearing plants, Every sort of fruit-bearing tree." And there it was. Earth produced green seed-bearing plants, all varieties, And fruit-bearing trees of all sorts. God saw that it was good. It was evening, it was morning— *Day Three.*

14-15

God spoke: "Lights! Come out! Shine in Heaven's sky! Separate Day from Night. Mark seasons and days and years, Lights in Heaven's sky to give light to Earth." And there it was.

16-19

God made two big lights, the larger to take charge of Day, the smaller to be in charge of Night; and he made the stars. God placed them in the heavenly sky to light up Earth and oversee Day and Night, to separate light and dark. God saw that it was good. It was evening, it was morning— *Day Four.*

20-23

God spoke: "Swarm, Ocean, with fish and all sea life! Birds, fly through the sky over Earth!" God created the huge whales, all the swarm of life in the waters, And every kind and species of flying birds. God saw that it was good. God blessed them: "Prosper! Reproduce! Fill Ocean! Birds, reproduce on Earth!" It was evening, it was morning—*Day Five.*

24-25

God spoke: "Earth, generate life! Every sort and kind: cattle and reptiles and wild animals—all kinds." And there it was: wild animals of every kind, Cattle of all kinds, every sort of reptile and bug. God saw that it was good.

26-28

God spoke: "Let us make human beings in our image, make them reflecting our nature So they can be responsible for the fish in the sea, the birds in the air, the cattle, And, yes, Earth itself, and every animal that moves on the face of Earth." God created human beings; he created them godlike, Reflecting God's nature. He created them male and female. God blessed them: "Prosper! Reproduce! Fill Earth! Take charge! Be responsible for fish in the sea and birds in the air, for every living thing that moves on the face of Earth."

29-30

Then God said, "I've given you every sort of seed-bearing plant on Earth and every kind of fruit-bearing tree, given them to you for food. To all animals and all birds, everything that moves and breathes, I give whatever grows out of the ground for food." And there it was.

31

God looked over everything he had made; it was so good, so very good! It was evening, it was morning— *Day Six*.
(Genesis 1:1-31 The Message) (14)

I have had many discussions down the years with friends who follow the Shepherd, over the details set out in the first chapter of Genesis, from those who believe in the literal twenty-four-hour day interpretation of the text, to those who believe the days were 'ages of creation' which could be thousands of years in length. Those who believe the literal term say that, "If you don't believe the literal translation of the words set out in Genesis, you can't believe anything else that you read in the Bible", and those on the other end of the spectrum arguing that "If you do believe the literal translation, then how do you hold in tension the age of the planet and the universe, as revealed by science, the dinosaurs or even the coal and oil under the earth's surface, which required fossils of every description to provide the raw material?"

I am no scientist, but the one thing I do know from Bible scholars that I trust, is that the Bible is not a science book, and shouldn't be read as one. It is a history book, and reading it as such, will bring life.

Jo and I together with our friends Derek and Glynis, had the privilege of staying for a few days with the geologist and writer John Wiester and his lovely wife on their cattle ranch in Buellton, California. John is the author of a book titled 'The Genesis Connection' in which he seeks to present the big picture of the major events in the history of the Cosmos, the planet Earth, and all life upon it.

I confess that when John was talking with us in the cool of the day, most of what he had to say went right over my head, but one thing stuck. It was a 'slap your forehead moment'.

John talked about time, and he used the example that he published in his book, to illustrate what he meant.

I copy it out verbatim for the reader, and trust that you too, will have a 'slap your forehead moment'.

To place key events and ages into a time frame we can more easily comprehend, let 5 billion years represent one year in discussing the history of the Universe and Earth. The history of the Universe and Earth would be three years in length.

Age of Universe Creation.

The creation of the Universe from the Big Bang to the formation of planet Earth would occupy two entire years on our relative time scale. The subsequent events in the history of the Earth would take place over the final period of one calendar year.

Age of Water Formation.

The final year would start 4.6 billion years ago when the Earth condensed from its nebular cloud of gas and dust particles. During January of this last year nothing of significance would happen. About the beginning of February, the Earth would start to outgas its primordial atmosphere of water vapour and carbon dioxide. With the arrival of March, the water vapour would begin condensing to form the Earth's first liquid water. By the end of March, the Earth would be covered by a shallow sea.

Age of Land Formation.

The first continental cratons would begin to appear at the end of March. By the middle of June, the era of great vertical movement in the Earth's crust would be essentially complete. Thereafter the Earth's crust would be divided into large continental cratons and interconnected deep ocean basins.

Age of Vegetation.

The age of blue-green algae would also begin at the end of March. It would dominate life until the arrival of October when more advanced forms of algae would appear.

Age of transformation of the Sun's Energy.

Photosynthesis of the blue-green algae would also begin at the end of March. It would not have an appreciable effect on the atmosphere until July 20. It would take from July 20 until October for enough free oxygen to accumulate to form the Earth's ozone screen. The Sun's energy would become increasingly beneficial to advanced forms of life.

Age of Marine Life.

About the middle of November, the Cambrian explosion of marine life would take place. Primitive fish would dominate the oceans by the end of the month.

Age of life on the Land and Man.

The age of Amphibians would begin on December 4, and reptiles would appear on December 15 until Christmas. About the end of Christmas Day, mammals would begin their explosive adaptive radiation. In less than a week familiar cattle, horses, dogs, and elephants would be present.

Cro-Magnon man would not appear on the calendar until six minutes before midnight on New Year's Eve! The beginning of agriculture and civilization-the appearance of modern man as we know him-would occur about one minute before midnight. About twelve seconds before midnight Christ would be born. The Industrial Revolution would last for about the final one second in this relative time history of planet Earth. (John L Wiester – The Genesis Connection) (21)

I don't begin to understand most of the proven science behind this, but all I can say is, 'What a Creator? Who else could do all of this by speaking a word?'

In his book, 'I am not but I Know I AM' (15) Louie Giglio writes the following thoughts about Creator God:

When He initiated the first ocean wave and carved out Earth's deepest canyons, forming the very dirt we call home, God intended that everything about it would point us back to Him. When He created the first man and woman, God wasn't obsessed with the glory of the human race, but with His own glory. (Louie Giglio – I am not but I know I AM)

As John says at the beginning of his Gospel,

1 In the beginning was the Word, and the Word was with God, and the Word was God. 2 He was with God in the beginning. 3 Through him all things were made; without him nothing was made that has been made. 4 In him was life, and that life was the light of all mankind. 5 The light shines in the darkness, and the darkness has not overcome it. (John 1:1-5 NIV)

From these disparate thoughts, I hope you can see what I see, that is that the Shepherd, who was intimately involved with everything that has ever been created, is passionate about His creation. As we are made in His image, is there anyone living who looks up at the sky at night and does not stare at the wonder of it all?

I believe the Shepherd is calling those who are far more intelligent than me, those of you who have the ability and intellect to fully understand how the cosmos works, to stand-up for Him and promote right understanding about this complex subject. This is, I believe, a calling for His followers who have deep knowledge of the various sciences, to work together to shed light on the enemy's schemes to undermine the truth of creation.

It is a calling for the rest of us to ensure that all of creation is looked after, whether it be the Earth that we live on, the animal kingdom, the plant life, the insect life, the natural resources above and below the earth and even Space. There is rubbish on and under the soil, the oceans are full of plastic of every description, and the sky is damaged in ways we have not yet understood. I hate to think what is happening in space, with all the derelict satellites spinning around the world! Let us keep those who govern our countries, informed about what we believe with regards to creation, and hold them to account for what they do with it in our name.

Listen to the voice of the Shepherd, and do what He asks you to do.

Questions:

1) Do you stand in awe when you see the wonders of creation? If not, ask the Shepherd to show you the wonders that He has created for you.

2) As you read scripture regarding creation, are you moved to speak on its behalf?

CHAPTER 5
JESUS THE GOOD SHEPHERD (JOHN 10:2-16)

As we have seen in Chapter Two, 'The Shepherd in the Old Testament', the prophet Ezekiel prophesies the following:

v.11 "I Myself will search for my sheep."

v.12 "I will look after my sheep."

v.13 "I will bring them out."

v.13 "I will pasture them."

v.14 "I will tend them."

v.15 "I will tend my sheep."

v.15 "I will have them lie down."

v.16 "I will search for the lost."

v.16 "I will...bring back the strays."

v.16 "I will...bind up the injured...."

V.16 "I will...strengthen the weak..."

(Ezekiel 34:11-16 NIV)

In John chapter ten, we see Jesus declaring to the Pharisees a description of Himself as the 'True Shepherd'. This statement enables us to see whether Ezekiel's prophecy was true or false.

1 "Very truly I tell you Pharisees, anyone who does not enter the sheep pen by the gate, but climbs in by some other way, is a thief and a robber. 2 The one who enters by the gate is the shepherd of the sheep. 3 The gatekeeper opens the gate for him, and the sheep listen to his voice. He calls his own sheep by name and leads them out. 4 When he has brought out all his own, he goes on ahead of them, and his sheep follow him because they know his voice. 5 But they will never follow a stranger; in fact, they will run away from him because they do not recognize a stranger's voice." 6 Jesus used this figure of speech, but the Pharisees did not understand what he was telling them.

7 Therefore Jesus said again, "Very truly I tell you, I am the gate for the sheep. 8 All who have come before me are thieves and robbers, but the sheep have not listened to them. 9 I am the gate; whoever enters through me will be saved. They will come in and go out, and find pasture. 10 The thief comes only to steal and kill and destroy; I have come that they may have life, and have it to the full. (John 10:1-9 NIV)

14 "I am the good shepherd; I know my sheep and my sheep know me— 15 just as the Father knows me and I know the Father—and I lay down my life for the sheep. 16 I have other sheep that are not of this sheep pen. I must bring them also. They too will listen to my voice, and there shall be one flock and one shepherd." (John 10:14-16 NIV)

Frankly, it doesn't need much persuasion to convince us that what the Shepherd Ezekiel is foretelling is indeed this Jesus of Nazareth, described by Himself as the 'Good Shepherd'.

Jesus says, "I am the good shepherd" twice in this passage. It is the fourth of seven "I am" declarations of Jesus recorded in John's Gospel. These

"I am" statements point to His unique, divine identity and purpose. It is good to remind ourselves of Jesus' "I am" declarations, so I have added them as an appendix at the end of this book.

It was right after declaring that He is "the gate" (or "door" as translated in other Bible versions) in John 10:7, that Jesus declares "I am the good shepherd." He is not only describing Himself as "the shepherd" but the "Good Shepherd."

As you continue to read this book, it is essential to understand that Jesus is 'the' good shepherd, not simply 'a' good shepherd, as others may be. Jesus is unique in character and can be trusted. (Psalm 23; Zechariah 13:7; Hebrews 13:20; 1 Peter 2:25; 1 Peter 5:4).

The Greek word used here for good is 'kalos'.

Strong's Number: 2570

Definition

Beautiful, handsome, excellent, eminent, choice, surpassing, precious, useful, suitable, commendable, admirable, beautiful to look at, shapely, magnificent, good, excellent in its nature and characteristics, and therefore well adapted to its ends

Genuine, approved, precious. joined to names of men designated by their office, competent, able, such as one ought to be.

Praiseworthy, noble, beautiful due to purity of heart and life.

This word signifies not only that which is good inwardly—character— but also that which is attractive outwardly. This outward attraction is not about looks. People can be very attractive on the surface, but scratch a little, and you may find something completely different. The outward attraction defined here is a beauty because of the inward life it reflects.

Using the phrase "the good shepherd," Jesus is referencing His inherent goodness, His righteousness, His beauty, His competence to do the job and His ability to carry out the Father's instructions. As shepherd of the sheep, He is the one who protects His flock, guides them to good pastures and nurtures and keeps them safe.

As Jesus declares that He is **'the gate for the sheep'** John 10:7, He is showing the contrast between Himself and the religious leaders, the Pharisees (John 10:12–13). He compares them to a "hired hand" who doesn't really care about the sheep. In John 10:10, Jesus speaks of thieves and robbers who sought to enter the sheepfold to steal, kill and destroy.

In John 10:12, the hired hand is contrasted with the True Shepherd who willingly gives up his life for the sheep. He who is a "hired hand" works for wages, which are his main consideration. His concern is not for the sheep but for himself.

The truth is that even if they were just "hired hands", they were still expected to exercise the same care and concern for the flock as the owners would. This was characteristic of a true shepherd.

The True Shepherd is the complete opposite to some of the "hired hands" that Jesus talks about, who thought only of themselves, as when a wolf appeared—the most common threat to sheep in that day—they abandoned the flock and fled, leaving the sheep to be scattered or killed. (John 10:12–13)

Today, God's earthly shepherds who have the care of God's people in their hands, are charged by the C.E.O. of the church to ensure that the flock is protected. Today, as in all of history, there is an enemy who seeks to devour the followers of the Shepherd, and it is the earthly shepherds job to seek the Shepherd, and ask Him what they must do to help His followers understand the plans of the enemy. We, as earthly shepherds, may not have to lay down our lives physically by fighting the enemy, but we should and must identify, with the help of the Holy Spirit, what he is trying to do to destroy lives.

To further prove what Jesus was saying, we read, 'just as the Son of Man did not come to be served, but to serve, and to give his life as a ransom for many'. (Matthew 20:28 NIV)

Through His willing sacrifice, Jesus made salvation possible for all who come to Him in faith. In proclaiming that He is the Good Shepherd, Jesus speaks of "laying down" His life for His sheep (John 10:15).

Jesus' death was divinely appointed. It is only through Him that we receive salvation. 'I am the good shepherd; I know my sheep and my sheep know me'. (John 10:14 NIV) More than this, Jesus makes it clear that it wasn't just for the Jews that he laid down His life, but also for 'the other sheep that are not of this sheep pen. I must bring them also. They too will listen to my voice, and there shall be one flock and one shepherd'. (John 10:16 NIV)

The 'other sheep' clearly refers to the non-Jews, that is the Gentiles. As a result, Jesus is the Good Shepherd over all, both Jew and Gentile, who come to believe upon Him (John 3:16), and therefore all who are made in the image of God, no matter their belief system, are now safe forever, if they would just acknowledge Him and have faith to follow the Shepherd.

Questions:

1) Do you know the 'True Shepherd'? If not, then His promise is, "If you search for Me, you will find Me". Why don't you look back over your life and see if you think knowing Him would have been helpful?

2) Do you feel safe in His care? If yes, your job is to find those who don't, and lead them to His safety. Why don't you name somebody you know right now and introduce them to Him?

3) Do you live with fear in your life? If yes, ask the Shepherd right now to show you His love, as perfect love casts out fear.

CHAPTER 6

THE YOUNG EARTHLY LIFE OF JESUS THE TRUE SHEPHERD

The Shepherd, during the last hours He spent with His disciples here on the earth, delivered for the rest of all time, His own very succinct understanding of His earthly life:

'First, I left the Father and arrived in the world; now I leave the world and travel to the Father'.

(John 16:28 The Message)

He came from the Father, the first stage; and back to the Father, the last; with 'come into the world' and 'leave the world' in between the two.

Heinrich August Wilhelm Meyer (10 January 1800 – 21 June 1873), was a German Protestant theologian, who observed that this remarkable statement of Jesus in John's gospel is **'a simple and grand summary of His entire personal life'.**

So, we start at the beginning. We can do this work with certainty, because of the gathering of eye-witness accounts recorded by Doctor Luke. My police officer friends tell me that there is nothing more powerful in a court case, than lots of independent eye witness statements supporting the prosecution's case. We don't know who Luke spoke to, to be able to write down his gospel stories, but we do know who he wrote to. He wrote to Theophilus to present 'an orderly account' of all that Jesus began to do and teach, and to ensure that he would have historical evidence of the life and times of the Saviour. The Shepherd and the Holy Spirit affirm this historical evidence for all time.

The story of Christmas is 'magical' to young children everywhere, and so it should be. Not that the story is magic in any way, but that it is a wonder that is 'magical'. I would say that this story ought to have the same effect on people of all ages, however, it is usually knocked out of us the minute we seem to understand things in a so-called logical way, and we lose the very essence of it. How can it possibly be true, ask most right-thinking people? No woman can conceive without a man doing his part, they argue, and of course in the natural realm this is correct. It is not possible.

What is impossible with man however, is completely possible with a Creator God, who out of nothing, created all things.

Let us look at Mary first and then Joseph.

Mary of Nazareth is history's most celebrated woman.

But Mary was not Divine; not sinless; and not the Mediator between God and man. Those titles belong to her Son, and her Son alone.

Moved by the Holy Spirit, Mary announces that "all generations would call her blessed". And so, we should. By God's grace, Mary became a woman worthy of our highest esteem and sincere imitation. We must remember Mary for all time.

Mary was of royal blood, able to trace her ancestry back to King David. But the House of David had fallen into disrepair. Herod now ruled over Israel, and Rome ruled over Herod. Thus Mary, who was a princess in Israel, was brought very low. Because of her lowly standing, she now lived with her family in the little town of Nazareth.

A good question for us is, has God been arbitrary in His choice of Mary to be that special person who would bring His Son into the world?

The answer to this question is absolutely not, because God makes His choices based upon certain qualities he sees in the people He chooses.

For the eyes of the Lord range throughout the earth to strengthen those whose hearts are fully committed to him. (2 Chronicles 16:9 NIV)

What is it that we know about Mary from Luke's gospel?
First, her father's name was Eli.
Second, she had a sister named Salome.
Third, she had a relative named Elizabeth.
Fourth, she is young.
Fifth, she is poor.
Sixth, she is a devout believer in God.
Seventh, she is very much in love.

Mary is a very real person in history and geography. She is not some figment of later writer's imagination. Mary has a family and she is 'known'.

When this amazing story opens, Mary is "betrothed" to Joseph, which means that she had formally agreed to marry him, but the "wedding" had not yet taken place. Between the "betrothal" and the "wedding feast" was a period usually lasting between six months to a year. During that period the couple were considered by all their friends and family to be married and were called husband and wife. During this period, they did not live together and did not consummate their marriage physically. The custom of that day meant that Mary would live with her parents and Joseph with his. Later, after the public wedding feast, Mary and Joseph would live together as husband and wife, in every way possible.

Having been through both of my daughters pre-wedding days and months, and seen how they coped, I guess that like my daughters and betrothed women everywhere, Mary could probably think of nothing else. Imagine that the wedding feast is still four or five months away, we can probably guess, correctly, that all her thoughts centred on the guest list, the decorations, the food, the music, and more importantly, what she will wear. Mary probably had never been happier. This must have been the most exciting time of her life. It certainly was for my two daughters.

What God asks Mary to do changes her future and her life forever.

Mary will be married, but not before rumours about her spread through the surrounding towns and villages. There will be a wedding feast, but not in the way she planned. It will all happen, but not the way this young woman would have wanted or expected.

Let's look at the story of what happens and see what Mary's response is?

26 In the sixth month of Elizabeth's pregnancy, God sent the angel Gabriel to Nazareth, a town in Galilee, 27 to a virgin pledged to be married to a man named Joseph, a descendant of David. The virgin's name was Mary. 28 The angel went to her and said, 'Greetings, you who are highly favoured! The Lord is with you.'

29 Mary was greatly troubled at his words and wondered what kind of greeting this might be. 30 But the angel said to her, 'Do not be afraid, Mary, you have found favour with God. 31 You will conceive and give birth to a son, and you are to call him Jesus. 32 He will be great and will be called the Son of the Most High. The Lord God will give him the throne of his father David, 33 and he will reign over Jacob's descendants for ever; his kingdom will never end.'

34 'How will this be,' Mary asked the angel, 'since I am a virgin?'

35 The angel answered, 'The Holy Spirit will come on you, and the power of the Most High will overshadow you. So the holy one to be born will be called the Son of God. 36 Even Elizabeth your relative is going to have a child in her old age, and she who was said to be

unable to conceive is in her sixth month. 37 For no word from God will ever fail.'

38 'I am the Lord's servant,' Mary answered. 'May your word to me be fulfilled.' Then the angel left her.
(Luke 1:26-38 NIV)

We need to see that Mary and Gabriel are about to have a conversation in which Gabriel does most of the talking. Gabriel says three different things to her, verse 28, that Mary is highly favoured and that the Lord is with her, in verses 30-33, that she was not to be afraid, that she would conceive and give birth to a son, and that this son will be great and will be called the Son of the 'Most High'. The Lord God will give him the throne of his father David, and He will reign over Jacob's descendants for ever; His kingdom will never end. Finally, in verses 35-37, Gabriel tells Mary that it is the Holy Spirit that will 'cover her', and to give her proof, Gabriel tells Mary about her relation, Elizabeth, who was unable to conceive but is now pregnant, and that she will give birth in her old age.

I can't imagine what Mary was thinking deep down in her heart when Gabriel said these things to her. I can't even imagine what she must have felt being confronted by this mighty angel. How would you have felt? The one thing we do know, is Mary's verbal response to him.

First, the reality of this meeting. Verse 29 sees Mary greatly troubled by the meeting and how Gabriel greets her, in verse 34, Mary asks, 'how can what you say be?' as she was a virgin, and then in verse 38, we begin to see how Mary starts to believe the impossible, when she says, 'I am the Lord's servant, may your word to me be fulfilled'.

The key point in this conversation between Gabriel and Mary, is the explanation of what is about to happen to her, will be the result of the direct intervention of God. The Holy Spirit is the agent of the Virgin Birth; overshadowing is the means of the Virgin Birth; the Son of God is the result of the Virgin Birth.

The fact is, that there really was no other way for Jesus to be born. I can't remember where I heard this, but a preacher once said, "Gabriel's words imply that the Virgin Birth was not just another Christmas miracle that God could have dispensed with had he so chosen. Without the Virgin Birth, there would be no Christmas at all." (Don't all practioner's of the Gospel wish that we could come up with statements like that?)

'I am the Lord's servant,' Mary answered. 'May your word to me be fulfilled.' Then the angel left her. (Luke 1:38 NIV)

I think we could probably call this one of the greatest statements of faith in the entire Bible. Mary first says yes to God, and she says Yes again to the seemingly impossible. Elsewhere in this book, I tell again and again the phrase that Mary said at the weeding feast in Cana, **'Whatever He tells you to do, do it'.** Can you see the echo of Mary's first response to God?

I talk about Mary before the Cross in more detail in Chapter 11, but I feel that what Jesus said to His mother at that time, needs to be said here.

25 Near the cross of Jesus stood his mother, his mother's sister, Mary the wife of Clopas, and Mary Magdalene. 26 When Jesus saw his mother there, and the disciple whom he loved standing nearby, he said to her, 'Woman, here is your son,' 27 and to the disciple, 'Here is your mother.' From that time on, this disciple took her into his home. (John 19:25-27 NIV)

So much love for His mother. Wonderful.

How about this statement, again from a preacher I have long forgotten, "Some of you have been saying to yourself, "God could never use me?" If you are not useable, you are dead right no matter how capable you are. If you are willing to make yourself useable, you are dead wrong." I love it.

Now for Joseph.

The Bible doesn't say much about Joseph, but there is much that we can find out about him.

Joseph was born in Bethlehem. We know that because he had to go back to his own town when the census was called.

Joseph was a carpenter. We know that, because Jesus carried on the same trade as his earthly father.

Joseph was a bachelor. We know that because he was betrothed to Mary.

Joseph was handpicked by God to be the foster father of Jesus. And that says enough.

There is little in the Bible of what Joseph said, but we have a pretty good understanding of what he did ... proving that a godly father is not just talk, but full of action!

We could sum up Joseph as someone who was a worker, someone who was reliable and most important of all, someone who was faithful.

When Joseph finds out that Mary is pregnant, and clearly not by him, he suffers in silence. There was no outward sulking to cover up his inner hurt, but he responds to the situation with a sense of justice and mercy towards Mary. His decision is to break the solemn engagement rather than live a lie. That is justice. For Mary's sake, he did it in private. That is mercy.

Joseph's story goes on. In Matthew's gospel, we read that:

19 Because Joseph her husband was faithful to the law, and yet did not want to expose her to public disgrace, he had in mind to divorce her quietly.

20 But after he had considered this, an angel of the Lord appeared to him in a dream and said, 'Joseph son of David, do not be afraid to take Mary home as your wife, because what is conceived in her is

from the Holy Spirit. 21 She will give birth to a son, and you are to give him the name Jesus, because he will save his people from their sins.'

22 All this took place to fulfil what the Lord had said through the prophet: 23 'The virgin will conceive and give birth to a son, and they will call him Immanuel' (which means 'God with us').

24 When Joseph woke up, he did what the angel of the Lord had commanded him and took Mary home as his wife. 25 But he did not consummate their marriage until she gave birth to a son. And he gave him the name Jesus.
(Matthew 1:19-25 NIV)

This time not a visible angel, but Joseph, through a dream, gets the same reassurance from heaven that Mary received. Joseph's response shows what a faithful follower of Yahweh he is.

Joseph, although clearly not a rich man, did his best for his young wife Mary, and their son. He did everything he could for them, including taking them to Egypt to protect their very lives. No horse, but a donkey, no Inn but a cattle stall! The young woman, Mary must have been frightened. If I were Joseph, I would have thought myself a failure as a husband and as a father.

The truth is he didn't fail. If you need proof, just look at how Mary and Jesus turn out under his care. His work as a carpenter was for Mary and Jesus. Joseph was ever present for his young family. Joseph did what God told him to do, and because of his faithfulness, Mary and the young Jesus survived.

The last thing Scripture says about Joseph is that Jesus was obedient to him and his mother Mary, and that Jesus grew in wisdom and stature.

47 Everyone who heard him was amazed at his understanding and his answers. 48 When his parents saw him, they were astonished. His

mother said to him, 'Son, why have you treated us like this? Your father and I have been anxiously searching for you.'

49 'Why were you searching for me?' he asked. 'Didn't you know I had to be in my Father's house?' 50 But they did not understand what he was saying to them.

51 Then he went down to Nazareth with them and was obedient to them. But his mother treasured all these things in her heart. 52 And Jesus grew in wisdom and stature, and in favour with God and man. (Luke 2:47-52 NIV)

When I first outlined this chapter in my mind, I didn't think that I would spend so much time on Mary and Joseph, but as I prayed about the subject of the early life of the Shepherd, I sensed that He wanted to remind the world about the wonderful news of Christmas. I also felt, and still do, that the Shepherd wants to make sure that we, as His followers, never forget, or worse, trivialise, his earthly mother and father, and He wants to remind us of how young they were, how frightened and afraid they were, and how courageous and full of faith they were.

The Shepherd is calling you right now to follow Him, and no matter what your age, He asks you to be bold and courageous, and follow Mary and Joseph's example, do what He asks you to do.

So, we follow Jesus from His lowly birth, to His young life.

On the surface, the books of Matthew and Luke seem to have different accounts of Jesus' birth and early life. How can we possibly see what is going on?

Matthew says Jesus was born in Bethlehem then sometime afterwards is taken to Egypt to escape Herod. After a period, his family decides to return to Bethlehem, but soon change their mind and travel to Nazareth instead.

According to Luke, however, Mary and Joseph were from Nazareth. They travel to Bethlehem because a census requires them to do so. While they are there Jesus is born in a manger. After his birth they wait for Mary to go through ritual purification, after which they travel to Jerusalem to sacrifice two birds at the temple. After the sacrifice they go home to Nazareth.

From my understanding, both accounts are correct because they speak of two different time periods.

I believe that the time sequence from Jesus' birth to Him being taken to Nazareth is as follows:

Joseph comes from the family of King David, and he was born in Bethlehem. The Romans, since before the birth of Jesus, required all people in Judea to return to their ancestral home so that they can be counted. Because of this decree Mary and Joseph travel to Bethlehem.

On the eighth day after his birth, Jesus is circumcised in accordance with the law of God.

After forty days of purification, as again required by God's law, Jesus is brought to Jerusalem's temple to be presented before God. His parents make an offering to the temple of two young birds. During their visit to the temple, a priest named Simeon, prophesies about Jesus' mission in His life, and then he blesses His parents Mary and Joseph.

Before Mary and Joseph leave the temple, a woman named Anna, a widowed prophetess who lived in the house of God, blesses them as well.

25 Now there was a man in Jerusalem called Simeon, who was righteous and devout. He was waiting for the consolation of Israel, and the Holy Spirit was on him. 26 It had been revealed to him by the Holy Spirit that he would not die before he had seen the Lord's Messiah. 27 Moved by the Spirit, he went into the temple courts. When the parents brought in the child Jesus to do for him what the

custom of the Law required, 28 Simeon took him in his arms and praised God, saying:

29 'Sovereign Lord, as you have promised, you may now dismiss your servant in peace.

30 For my eyes have seen your salvation, 31 which you have prepared in the sight of all nations:

32 a light for revelation to the Gentiles, and the glory of your people Israel.'

33 The child's father and mother marvelled at what was said about him. 34 Then Simeon blessed them and said to Mary, his mother: 'This child is destined to cause the falling and rising of many in Israel, and to be a sign that will be spoken against, 35 so that the thoughts of many hearts will be revealed. And a sword will pierce your own soul too.'

36 There was also a prophet, Anna, the daughter of Penuel, of the tribe of Asher. She was very old; she had lived with her husband seven years after her marriage, 37 and then was a widow until she was eighty-four. She never left the temple but worshipped night and day, fasting and praying. 38 Coming up to them at that very moment, she gave thanks to God and spoke about the child to all who were looking forward to the redemption of Jerusalem.
(Luke 2:25-38 NIV)

The Wise Men, or 'Magi', from the East, arrive in Jerusalem a year or more after Jesus is born, with the aim of asking Herod where the child is living. Although Herod does not have a clue of where the Messiah was to be born he asks the priests and scribes of the day if they knew. They tell Herod the Christ would be born in Bethlehem. After leaving Jerusalem the Wise Men, or Magi, follow the same star that brought them to Judea. When they arrive at the place of His birth they see Mary and Jesus, and offer their gifts.

9 After they had heard the king, they went on their way, and the star they had seen when it rose went ahead of them until it stopped over the place where the child was. 10 When they saw the star, they were overjoyed. 11 On coming to the house, they saw the child with his mother Mary, and they bowed down and worshipped him. Then they opened their treasures and presented him with gifts of gold, frankincense and myrrh.
(Matthew 2:9-11 NIV)

After the wise men leave to return home, an angel of the Lord tells Joseph, in a dream, to flee to Egypt, as Herod wants to kill their child.

13 When they had gone, an angel of the Lord appeared to Joseph in a dream. 'Get up,' he said, 'take the child and his mother and escape to Egypt. Stay there until I tell you, for Herod is going to search for the child to kill him.'

14 So he got up, took the child and his mother during the night and left for Egypt, 15 where he stayed until the death of Herod. And so was fulfilled what the Lord had said through the prophet: 'Out of Egypt I called my son'.
(Matthew 2:13-15 NIV)

Herod sends out a command that, in Bethlehem and the surrounding area, all male children aged two years and younger, should be put to death.

16 When Herod realised that he had been outwitted by the Magi, he was furious, and he gave orders to kill all the boys in Bethlehem and its vicinity who were two years old and under, in accordance with the time he had learned from the Magi. 17 Then what was said through the prophet Jeremiah was fulfilled:

18 'A voice is heard in Ramah, weeping and great mourning, Rachel weeping for her children and refusing to be comforted, because they are no more'.
(Matthew 2:16-18 NIV)

I can only imagine what Father God was feeling at this time. All those children, all those broken-hearted mothers, all that pain.

The Shepherd today is reminding us of all the young lives that are destroyed in wars, in poverty and in hunger and abuse, and He also asks us to be mindful of life that is destroyed in the wombs of young women around the world. If you take the time to listen, you will hear weeping in heaven today for all that lost young life, and the human pain that goes with it.

Back to the story. After Herod dies an angel of the Lord once more appears to Joseph in a dream, and tells him it is now safe to return to Israel. Fearful of going back to live in Bethlehem, Joseph again has an angelic being instruct him to go to Nazareth.

19 After Herod died, an angel of the Lord appeared in a dream to Joseph in Egypt 20 and said, 'Get up, take the child and his mother and go to the land of Israel, for those who were trying to take the child's life are dead.'

21 So he got up, took the child and his mother and went to the land of Israel. 22 But when he heard that Archelaus was reigning in Judea in place of his father Herod, he was afraid to go there. Having been warned in a dream, he withdrew to the district of Galilee, 23 and he went and lived in a town called Nazareth. So was fulfilled what was said through the prophets, that he would be called a Nazarene.

Jesus now lives in Nazareth, up until the beginning of his public ministry, at which time he will move to Capernaum.
(Matthew 2:19-23 NIV)

When Joseph and Mary had done everything required by the Law of the Lord, they returned to Galilee to their own town of Nazareth. (Luke 2:39 NIV)

Why the need for all the detail you may ask? Just like some of the things written today about Mary and Joseph, there seems to be a tendency amongst some, to say that it is all irrelevant in today's modern world. It was all so long ago, and is it important in the overall scheme of things? The written detailed history shows that it is.

Just like the need for the world to know the truth about The Shepherd's earthly mother and father, so does it need to know the truth about the lead-up to all that Jesus did, here on the earth. The King of Heaven, left His Father and lived on the earth as a man, and was brought up by loving earthly parents. Even though He was born with a price on His head, for at least two years, along with Mary and Joseph, He lived as an immigrant in a foreign land. The Shepherd knows what it is like to be a refugee.

Now we can look at the first time the Shepherd, as it were, started to reveal, and therefore confirm, to Mary and Joseph who He was. I think that it could be very easy in the busyness of life to forget over time, all the wonderful, crazy promises made to Mary and Joseph by various angels in person and in dreams, and although the Bible is silent on this matter, I can't help feeling that the following conversation between Jesus and Mary and Joseph, and especially Mary, would have been a timely reminder.

47 Everyone who heard him was amazed at his understanding and his answers. 48 When his parents saw him, they were astonished. His mother said to him, 'Son, why have you treated us like this? Your father and I have been anxiously searching for you.'

49 'Why were you searching for me?' he asked. 'Didn't you know I had to be in my Father's house?'
(Luke 2:47:49 NIV)

It would be so easy to spend time delving into the whole story - a lost child, (who hasn't suffered that fate at some time in their life?), journeys back and forth along very dangerous roads, and reconciliations – but we must major on what the young Shepherd was doing in all of this.

Look where these concerned parents find their little boy? Jesus was in the temple, sitting among the scholars and teachers. The only place where such a group of scholars and teachers would have gathered, would have probably been where they always talked and studied together, that is in the temple grounds.

What could possibly have been happening? Here is this young boy, and He is amazing the scholars and teachers with His grasp of the things of God. It seems that both His questions and His answers reveal a depth of wisdom well beyond His years. It doesn't say, but presumably Jesus was a good and diligent student back at His own home in Nazareth, and now that He is at the Temple in Jerusalem, the very Centre of Jewish thought and wisdom, He poses some questions that leave His hearers speechless.

When Mary and Joseph found Jesus among the scholars and teachers, I wonder if they ran in and interrupted the discussions happening between them. Oh, to have been a fly on the wall! These men were the very elite of Jewish life, and I am not sure that if it was me, whether I would have rushed in or just stood quietly on the side-lines until a lull came in their conversation?

I know – this is completely irrelevant, but I just wonder.

Mary pushes forward, like only a mother can, and asks her son these tender words, "Son, why have you treated us like this?" I have vivid memories of my mum, when, after I went missing, shouting, "Where have you been. I was worried sick." My mum shouted out of anger at first, and then relief when she knew that I was okay. I have a sneaky suspicion that Mary did the same.

What Mary was saying was, "did you not stop to think about how concerned we would be about you?" Mary and Joseph would have been consumed with grief, looking frantically for the child that God had placed in their care.

At first sight, Jesus' response may sound to be a bit lacking in respect, but it was both a respectful and true response to the questions.

The reality was that there was no need for Mary and Joseph to look for Him; in Jesus' view, they should have known that if He was not with them, He would be busy with the things of His Heavenly Father.

This is where we see, for the first time, that Jesus revealed His identity. What must He have been thinking? Maybe He was seeing for the first time since leaving His Glory in Heaven, how man was interpreting His Father's instructions. Who knows, but Jesus.

Mary had said to her young son, '**Your father and I have been looking for you all over the place**'.

Jesus' answer was clear. He was telling them that He must be about His Father's business. Joseph was not Jesus' real father, God was, and now that Jesus is becoming a man, He must move his loyalty and submission from his earthly parents to His Father in heaven.

Being about His Father's business did not preclude Him from living obediently in the home of Joseph and Mary. The Man who was God, lived with and obeyed all that a flawed mother and step-dad asked of Him.

If Jesus, who was perfect, submitted himself completely to imperfect parents, how much more must we submit our imperfect lives to our perfect heavenly Father?

Questions:

1) **What and who governs your life?**

2) **What is the driving force that gets you up in the mornings?**

   The answer to these two questions will reveal to you what god you are serving, and by association, where your eternal destiny lies.

CHAPTER 7
THE SHEPHERD AT WORK

From the previous chapters, I hope you can see that there are clearly benefits from listening and consequences for ignoring the voice of the Shepherd.

If you read the parables set out in Matthew, Mark and Luke, you will find that at least thirty-two of them mention a work-related activity. Jesus has work on His mind and in His thinking. This must come as no surprise, on the basis that before time, He created everything.

So, let's see Him at work.

At the very beginning of man's journey with God, after **God created mankind in His own image, in the image of God He created them; male and female He created them.** (Genesis 1:27 NIV) God gave instructions to Adam and Eve to be fruitful, multiply, fill the earth and subdue it; have dominion over fish in the sea, birds of the air and every living thing that moves on the earth. God also walked with Adam and Eve in the garden and presumably discussed all that they were doing on his behalf in that wonderful place. They must have felt safe and secure. This is a picture of the Shepherd ensuring the safety and harmony of people who were made in His image.

After this comes the fall of all mankind, a subject not for this book, but the reason for all that scripture reveals about how essential it is for mankind to seek the Shepherd's voice.

Later in the story of God and His people, we hear about the various covenants that He instigates with Abraham, Isaac, and Jacob, and then the miraculous in the stories of the deliverance of His people Israel from Egypt, the journey through the desert including the giving of the Law, the Ten Commandments and the miraculous provision of food and water, the crossing of the Red Sea, and the Glory of the Lord filling first the Tent of Meeting and then ultimately the Temple.

All this showing the Shepherd of Israel is hard at work looking after His flock.

As the Beatles would sing..........

> ### *LOVE*
> #### *LOVE*
> ##### *LOVE*

John White, in his wonderful practical handbook for Christian living, titled 'The Fight' (4), helpfully says this about the voice of the Shepherd:

Scripture emphasizes the presence of a Guide (Shepherd) rather than techniques for being guided (Shepherded). "My presence will go with you, and I will give you rest." We are meant to enjoy the subjective experiences of comfort, reassurance and fellowship with God. The fact that some Christians allow themselves to be deceived, confusing the voice of their own desires with the voice of the Shepherd, must not make us retreat from the assertion that God has promised guidance as well as the experience of fellowship with Him while He is guiding us. We are not meant to grope in mists and darkness for the way. Nor are we meant to tread it alone.

Yet if other Christians can be fooled, what is to prevent us from being fooled?

When Jesus said, "My sheep hear My voice," we correctly interpret Him to say, "My sheep can distinguish My voice." But that is not all He is saying. The word used implies "My sheep pay heed to

My voice." The sheep is not concerned about losing the way. The Shepherd knows the right way and will make sure the sheep is taken care of. What does concern the sheep is that he obeys the Shepherd's commands.

John White goes on to say:

If I but concern myself with hearing the voice of the Shepherd, paying heed to Christ, obeying Him, doing His will, I shall find that the problem of distinguishing His voice will begin to take care of itself.

I have seen Eastern shepherds at work in Cyprus, Romania and Bulgaria, and it is clear to me that although sheep do seem to be rather stupid and easily led, with this type of shepherd, they feel safe when they hear their voice, and will follow where ever they lead them.

The opposite seems to be the case, although I am sure that there are exceptions, when we see shepherds from the West moving their sheep. Almost without exception, the shepherds need the assistance of sheepdogs to get the sheep on the move and keep them from wandering off into danger.

If I was a sheep, I know which type of shepherd I would want to lead me to good food. The one I had grown to recognise and trust, rather than the one that uses dogs yapping at my heels.

My elder daughter, Victoria, when she was younger, had a Saturday job working in a local school on their small farm, and part of her job was to move a small flock of sheep to new pasture. Without fail, while she was at the school, Jo and I would get a phone call to say that the sheep were out, and she couldn't get them to go where they should go. So, we would go over and try to help move them in the right direction, which seemed to take forever. The sheep didn't know who we were and every time we approached them, they would scatter.

I know it didn't help that we didn't know what we were doing, but none the less, the story helps to reveal some truths about hearing the voice of the Shepherd.

Today, there are so many voices speaking into our hearts and minds, that it can be difficult, to say the least, to distinguish who is saying what and then how we should respond to them.

It is not the subject of this book to delve into the questions surrounding this statement, but it is my intention to guide the reader in how to recognise the voice of the Shepherd at work in your life.

As mentioned elsewhere, the Bible is the authorative, infallible Word of God in written form, and everything we hear should be tested against it.

The Shepherd's words will always reflect, in every way, the words revealed to us in scripture. The senses behind the words that the Shepherd speaks will drip with love and encouragement. Over time, if you continue to listen, you will begin to recognise when it is Him and not another. The Shepherd will not ask you to commit something that goes against His word, the Bible, nor will He ask you to go against His teaching. He may well ask you to do things outside of your experience or your comfort zone, but His promise is that He will always be with you, until the very end of time.

Unfortunately, my limited experience tells me that whenever I decide to follow His call, it seems that amongst the first voices that rise to try and stop me are those of fellow followers of Jesus, who with the best of intentions, can only see the down-side of doing whatever it is I am called to do.

The Shepherd is always at work, and He is looking for those who will hear what He has to say, and in Mary's words, "do it".

There is nothing better this side of Heaven, apart from doing the works of the One who has called us.

I love churches where the people believe whole heartedly that Jesus is indeed the True Shepherd, and that His commands are full of truth and full of Heaven. Truly, mountains can be moved if only we have faith the size of a mustard seed, and I love to be with people who passionately believe this.

Questions:

1) What would you like to see Jesus do, maybe in your family, or in your school, or in your workplace, or in your community?

2) How could you distinguish the voice of the Shepherd from all the other voices that might seek to guide you?

CHAPTER 8

THE SHEPHERD AND PROVISION

Ever since I made the decision to follow Jesus, I have had a feeling that He would never let me down, especially regarding my family, and if I put Him first in my life, He would use me for His glory. I do not say that if I didn't put Him first, He could not use me, as He is Lord and He can do whatever He wants, but it seemed clear to me that this was what He wanted of me.

I am forever grateful for so many leaders who have said, "God first, family second and church third". I tell everyone who is prepared to listen that this is the best way to live a full, contented, and safe life.

From my first understanding of scripture, even the baby steps taken at the beginning of my walk with the Shepherd, I have been captivated by the things Jesus did regarding provision. I am certain that what Jesus did over two thousand years ago, is the key to provision today.

In one of my quiet times with the Shepherd, I was reminded of these verses in Psalm 50:

'But why should I want your blue-ribbon bull, or more and more goats from your herds?

Every creature in the forest is mine, the wild animals on all the mountains.

I know every mountain bird by name; the scampering field mice are my friends'.
(Psalm 50:9-11 The Message)

I thought, I know what this means. I had heard many sermons on this Psalm from some amazingly clever preachers, and as I was about to dismiss the thought as a reminder of them, I sensed the Shepherd say, "Yes, it is true that I own the cattle on a thousand hills, and everything you have heard is correct. However, please do not miss the fact that I own the thousand hills that the cattle graze on." I have never forgotten that interaction with the Shepherd. Everything belongs to Him. He has all the resources that we need as His followers, to do the work that He has called us to do.

The Shepherd gives a timely word to all church leaders who doubt this statement. To those who keep asking their people to give more and more of their financial resources to enable this or that mission, to those who would charge people to hear the gospel, and especially to those whose lifestyle doesn't reflect that of the Shepherd – 'RESOURCES FOLLOW VISION'. The Shepherd is talking about the resources of Heaven being released to enable the vision of Heaven to be accomplished. Like many of you church leaders, I have heard again and again from people who don't yet know the Shepherd, the phrase "All they are after is your money!" Remember, 'Freely you have received, freely give'.

Before I go on, I must recall two wonderful provision stories in the Old Testament. One concerning Elijah and the other, Elisha. I encourage you to read and study these two stories, which reflect first the goodness of God, and secondly the obedience of God's servants.

7 Sometime later the brook dried up because there had been no rain in the land. 8 Then the word of the Lord came to him: 9 'Go at once to Zarephath in the region of Sidon and stay there. I have instructed a widow there to supply you with food.' 10 So he went to Zarephath.

When he came to the town gate, a widow was there gathering sticks. He called to her and asked, 'Would you bring me a little water in a jar, so I may have a drink?' 11 As she was going to get it, he called, 'And bring me, please, a piece of bread.'

12 'As surely as the Lord your God lives,' she replied, 'I don't have any bread – only a handful of flour in a jar and a little olive oil in a jug. I am gathering a few sticks to take home and make a meal for myself and my son, that we may eat it – and die.'

13 Elijah said to her, 'Don't be afraid. Go home and do as you have said. But first make a small loaf of bread for me from what you have and bring it to me, and then make something for yourself and your son. 14 For this is what the Lord, the God of Israel, says: "The jar of flour will not be used up and the jug of oil will not run dry until the day the Lord sends rain on the land."'

15 She went away and did as Elijah had told her. So, there was food every day for Elijah and for the woman and her family. 16 For the jar of flour was not used up and the jug of oil did not run dry, in keeping with the word of the Lord spoken by Elijah.
(1 Kings17:7-16 NIV)

1 The wife of a man from the company of the prophets cried out to Elisha, 'Your servant my husband is dead, and you know that he revered the Lord. But now his creditor is coming to take my two boys as his slaves.'

2 Elisha replied to her, 'How can I help you? Tell me, what do you have in your house?'

'Your servant has nothing there at all,' she said, 'except a small jar of olive oil.'

3 Elisha said, 'Go around and ask all your neighbours for empty jars. Don't ask for just a few. 4 Then go inside and shut the door behind

you and your sons. Pour oil into all the jars, and as each is filled, put it to one side.'

5 She left him and shut the door behind her and her sons. They brought the jars to her and she kept pouring. 6 When all the jars were full, she said to her son, 'Bring me another one.'

But he replied, 'There is not a jar left.' Then the oil stopped flowing.

7 She went and told the man of God, and he said, 'Go, sell the oil and pay your debts. You and your sons can live on what is left.'
(2 Kings 4:1-7 NIV)

My own excitement regarding provision, started with the 'turning water in to wine' story at the wedding feast in Cana, revealed in the book of John chapter 2. Basically, the bridegroom had underestimated the amount of wine that was needed for the feast, so Jesus tells the servants to use the water reserved for ceremonial washing, by pouring it into jars, and delivering amazing wine to the guests.

I have heard all sorts of arguments and sermons about this story and what it might mean.

The timing, the setting and the reasons behind the story seem to have been a subject that people down the ages wanted to dissect and maybe find some hidden meaning, or as Tom Wright says in his 'John for Everyone Part One' book (5), **some think these are things that didn't actually happen, but which illustrate some supposedly deeper, more 'spiritual' truth.**

For me as a practioner, I fully accept and would commend what Tom Wright goes on to say about this 'Sign' and provision miracle in his book – **It is about transformation: The different dimension of reality that comes into being when Jesus is present and when, as Mary, His mother, tells the servants, people do whatever Jesus tells them.**

Further in his understanding of this text, Tom Wright says, **the wedding is a foretaste of the great Heavenly feast in store for God's people (Revelation 21:2). The water-jars, used for Jewish purification rites, are a sign that God is doing a new thing from within the old Jewish system, bringing purification to Israel and the World in a whole new way.**

All of this is wonderful and enlightening and very encouraging.

But I believe that there is also a very human side to this story.

As a dad who has walked both his daughters 'Up the aisle' for their weddings, if I couldn't have provided for their party afterwards, I would have felt rather sad, and although neither of the parties were extravagant, Jo and I were able to do our best for them.

Please note that this is not an argument for a prosperity gospel, nor indeed for huge debt or wealthy parents – It is a desire to be as generous as we can be, given limited resources, all in response to a very generous Saviour.

I can almost see the anguish on the faces of the parents at this wedding in Cana, doing their very best but struggling to provide as the party went on. In the turmoil, the Shepherd sees what is happening, and alongside all that Tom Wright says, Jesus provides the very thing that the family need. As a speaker said, whose name I have forgotten, "The best wine in the whole of the universe was provided on that day". Wow!

I write elsewhere about 'Kingdom Provision', but I just want to add here that I am absolutely convinced that this was not man-made wine that was improved, it was a supernatural wine, a gift straight from Heaven.

There are four other significant miracles of provision found in the books of Matthew, Mark, Luke and John. These are the 'Feeding of the 5,000', (Matthew 14:15-21; Mark 6:35-44) 'The Feeding of the 4,000, (Matthew 15:32-38; Mark 8:1-9) 'The catch of fish', (Luke 5:4-11) and 'The further catch of fish'. (John 21:1-11.)

As an aside, the miracles relating to feeding, I am certain, are key to providing food for the hungry of the world today. If man won't feed the multitudes because of greed or financial gain, then the church should follow the ways of the Shepherd and with compassion for the hungry – feed them.

The first of the two occasions show clearly that there were 5,000 males. Matthew further emphasises the point by adding **'besides women and children'**. (Matthew 14-21 NIV)

This crowd is clearly enormous. The NIV Study Bible (10) helpfully tells us that, **the crowd is amazing in the light of the fact that the neighbouring towns of Capernaum and Bethsaida probably had a population of 2,000 – 3,000 each.**

It is beyond all earthly understanding that 'Five loaves and two fish' could feed such a multitude.

If Jesus was indeed, as He claimed to be, God with us, the miracle presents no difficulties for Him whatsoever.

God had promised the Jewish forefathers that "When the True Shepherd came, the desert would become rich pasture where the sheep would be gathered and fed (Ezekiel 34:23-31), and here the Messiah does exactly that. Jesus is the True Shepherd who provides for all our needs so that we lack nothing. (Psalm 23:1)

I talked in the Introduction to this book about a second 'dream/vision' that I sensed the Shepherd had given me, which had the title, 'Village Aid'. I was concerned at the time about the constant requests that came through the front door of both the church and our home, from Christian Charities, asking for money for this or that initiative that they were involved in. I wasn't concerned about the charities, who were clearly doing wonderful work around the world, just as Jesus told us to do, it was about the seemingly continuing lack of funding to carry out the work that concerned me. I knew then, and still do today, that resources will always follow a Godly vision, so the disparity between the two became the basis of my prayer life at that time. It was into this prayer life that I had the 'dream/vision'.

I was reminded about what the Shepherd did when He fed the 5,000 and the 4,000. He took what they had, prayed over it and then told His followers to distribute the food.

The basis of 'Village Aid' was – give what you have, if only a pound, pray over it, give thanks for it, then do what the Shepherd tells you to do with it.

I saw in my mind's eye, six million followers of the Shepherd, giving Him six million pounds, and watching in awe as the money was multiplied to meet the needs of the day.

It just seemed so simple and so biblical.

Unfortunately, the leaders of the church I was in at the time thought that it was probably too simplistic, and suggested that I do nothing with it. To my shame and embarrassment, I just put it all to one side, and left it there. I don't know if this is just a rant or the Shepherd reinstating the 'vision/dream', but one thing is for certain – the Saviour of the world is more than capable of taking the little that we can give Him and turning it into everything that is needed to fulfil the calling of the church.

So, with that in mind, we continue with the Shepherd and provision:

The second miracle, and it is indeed separate from the first, as confirmed by Jesus Himself in Mark 8:18 & 19, **'Why are you talking about having no bread? Do you still not see or understand? Are your hearts hardened? Do you have eyes but fail to see, and ears but fail to hear? And don't you remember? When I broke the five loaves for the five thousand, how many basketfuls of pieces did you pick up? The disciples answered, "Seven"".** Jesus said to them, **'Do you still not understand?'** (N I V)

These are indeed miracles.

I urge you, please reader, do not let anybody try to mislead you into believing that these are just stories to support spiritual theories. The Shepherd has all the resources that you need, if only you will listen to His voice, and do what He says.

The story of the third miracle recorded in Luke 5:1-11 is important for those of us who do, however dimly, listen to the Shepherd. It undergirds the promises of God when we do as He asks.

Looking back into history, it is difficult for us today to understand exactly what was going on in the minds of Jesus' followers. Remember that those first followers of Jesus didn't have the full story. They knew the scriptures inside out, they were with Jesus and they saw the miracles coming about by His command, and they almost certainly believed in their hearts that Jesus was who He said He was. But, can we say that they truly understood all that was going on?

In this story, we find Simon Peter in his fishing boat, putting out into the lake a little way from land so that Jesus could teach the multitudes that had followed Him from the safety of the boat.

Simon Peter had just handed over his greatest possession, his boat, to Jesus, so that He could continue in His work of preaching the Good News.

At this time in history and geography, this was the greatest need that Jesus had. He needed a platform, and Simon Peter seemed happy for his boat to be used.

It is good to remember that Simon Peter's boat, together with his nets, was all that he had to enable him to provide for his family.

Having finished His talk, Jesus then says to Simon Peter, **'Put out into deep water, and let down your nets for a catch'**. (Luke 5:4 N I V)

Here comes the debate and then final acceptance. Simon Peter says to Jesus, **'Master, we've worked hard all night and haven't caught**

anything. But because you say so, I will let down the nets'. (Luke 5:5 N I V)

These fishermen of the lake were the best fishermen of their time – they had learnt their craft, which was handed down from father to son, and more than that, they knew all there was to know about the lake and where the fish were likely to be found.

They had caught nothing. They were tired. What was the point in going back to fish?

They hadn't learnt in full that when the Shepherd speaks, He backs up what He says with everything He has at His disposal. (Remember if you can – In the beginning of all things, there was nothing, and into that nothingness, He created the universe!)

None the less, this wonderful man, Simon Peter says, "Because you say so, I will let down the nets". (An echo again of what Mary said to the servants.)

Two things happen now. The first is that their need for fish to make a living is provided, and the second is to see that Jesus is indeed who He says He is.

The provision miracle answers both needs.

The fourth miracle found in John 21:1-11, happens after Jesus' crucifixion and resurrection, and the commissioning of the apostles.

I have heard many different thoughts about why Simon Peter decided to go back to sea and fish. From disappointment through to maybe a sense of unworthiness because of his denial of Jesus, and probably everything between.

I am sure that there will be truth in all the different understandings of why Simon Peter did this, and as I have stated at the beginning of this book, I am a practioner of the Gospel and not a theologian, however, these approaches to what was going on don't satisfy my questioning as to why he would go back to sea and fish after the resurrection and commissioning.

I am not saying that people are wrong to teach in the way described above, but could there be something different happening here?

My experience of leading teams into the mission field, has shown me that when the task given to us by Jesus is finished, there always seems to be a sense of loss. When on the mission field, the reliance on the Shepherd's voice is critical, as I mentioned before with my friend John in Bulgaria, so when the task is finished, I believe a sense of loss is felt, in that we can go back to whatever field we have been trained in, and at that point, we may feel that we don't need the same level of guidance that we have got used to on the mission itself.

Could this be what Simon Peter is feeling? Could he be thinking, "I am good at this, so I don't need so much help".

I leave this thought for those who understand these things more than I do.

The lesson I believe this 'Provision Miracle' shows us is that even in the place where we live and work, maybe where we have been ably trained by good teachers or even where we are naturally gifted, the Shepherd wants us to know that He can speak into the situations we find ourselves in, and if we listen to His voice and obey His commands, as Simon Peter and the others did, then the outcome should convince us that Jesus really is indeed who He says He is, and that He will release 'Provision Miracles' into the life that we lead.

Never forget our job description:

26 Those who consider themselves religious and yet do not keep a tight rein on their tongues deceive themselves, and their religion is worthless. 27 Religion that God our Father accepts as pure and

faultless is this: to look after orphans and widows in their distress and to keep oneself from being polluted by the world.
(James 1:26-27 NIV)

And:

6 He is the Maker of heaven and earth, the sea, and everything in them – he remains faithful for ever.

7 He upholds the cause of the oppressed and gives food to the hungry. The Lord sets prisoners free,

8 the Lord gives sight to the blind, the Lord lifts up those who are bowed down, the Lord loves the righteous.

9 The Lord watches over the foreigner and sustains the fatherless and the widow, but he frustrates the ways of the wicked.

10 The Lord reigns for ever, your God, O Zion, for all generations.

(Psalm 146:6-10 NIV)

All the resources of heaven are available to us today to enable us to fulfil the work that the Shepherd calls us to do.

I believe the Shepherd would say to church leaders, "stop looking to man to provide what you need to carry out what He is calling you to do. The resources that you need are waiting to be released to you, if only you would ask the Shepherd for them."

I know the transition can be difficult, I have been there myself, however, I also know from experience that this is the only key that opens up the resources of heaven.

I believe that the Shepherd has much more to say about this. About church buildings that are unused most days of the week, about asking man to provide funds for the homeless, for food banks and for other caring ministries that the Shepherd is calling us to help Him with, selling tickets for people to hear the gospel (Freely you have received, freely give!), and much, much more. This is not for this book, and might not even be for me, but this subject will come to the fore sooner or later.

So, provision? It is all readily available, if only we would ask.

I hear the echo of my friend Terry, when he said, "It's ok, everything we believe is real".

Questions:

1) How has all the training you have had together with your experience of life shown you that His provision is enough for every situation that you might find yourself in?

2) What does your spirit do when you hear about supernatural miracles? Is this something that you yearn to see and experience in your own life?

3) How would you like to see the resources of heaven released here on the earth?

CHAPTER 9

THE SHEPHERD AND THE FATHER

Having studied all that Jesus did here on the earth, it is clear to me that at the very centre of His life & ministry was His relationship with His Father.

John's Gospel shows us just how true this is.

'As the Father has loved me, so have I loved you. Now remain in my love'. (John 15:9 NIV)

Jesus loves us because the Father loves Him – this is because the source of all love is the Father Himself.

As a man walking and living on the earth, Jesus displayed and lived out His life in full obedience to His Heavenly Father all the days of His life.

'For as the Father has life in Himself, so he has granted the Son also to have life in Himself'. (John 5:26 NIV)

The Bible states that all who believe in and follow the Shepherd are 'in Christ', and therefore now have that same life within us, because the New Testament clearly shows that the flow of life is from the Father to the Son, and then on through the Son to all who believe and follow Him.

Jesus' nature & character was that of His Father.

The Son is the radiance of God's glory and the exact representation of his being, sustaining all things by his powerful word. (Hebrews 1:3 NIV)

It must have been almost impossible for those who followed the Shepherd at the time, let alone the Pharisees, to understand that the God who created all things out of nothing, was living and walking amongst them. For some today, it still seems to be impossible for them to grasp the wonderful truth of who Jesus is.

We are reminded in the following passage of scripture, that by the transforming work of the Holy Spirit, all who follow the Shepherd are being changed into His likeness.

'And we all, who with unveiled faces contemplate the Lord's glory, are being transformed into his image with ever-increasing glory, which comes from the Lord, who is the Spirit'. (2 Corinthians 3:18 NIV)

Jesus' work was His Father's work, His mission and His purpose were His Father's mission and purpose, His prayer life was centred on His Father, and even the cup of suffering in Gethsemane was His Father's cup.

First, His work:

"So Jesus said, "When you have lifted up the Son of Man, then you will know that I am he and that I do nothing on my own but speak just what the Father has taught me".
(John 8:28 NIV)

49 "For I did not speak on my own, but the Father who sent me commanded me to say all that I have spoken. 50 I know that his command leads to eternal life. So whatever I say is just what the Father has told me to say." (John 12:49-50 NIV)

"Don't you believe that I am in the Father, and that the Father is in me? The words I say to you I do not speak on my own authority. Rather, it is the Father, living in me, who is doing his work." (John 14:10 NIV)

"For I gave them the words you gave me and they accepted them. They knew with certainty that I came from you, and they believed that you sent me". (John 17:8 NIV)

If you study the life and times of the Shepherd, it is not long before you come across the many miracles that He performs, and as you read His words, it is impossible not to see the love that He had for the people around Him, whether it was by a word of encouragement or a word of admonishment.

It seems to me that the miracles are key for the understanding of the followers of the Shepherd in those days, and if we approach the miracles with an open heart and mind, it will be the same for us today.

Look at them:

Healing –

Man with leprosy, roman centurion's servant, Peter's mother-in-law, two men from Gadara, paralysed man, woman with bleeding, two blind men, man mute and possessed, man with a shrivelled hand, man blind, mute and possessed, Canaanite woman's daughter, boy with a demon, two blind men (one named), deaf mute, man possessed, blind man at Bethsaida, crippled woman, man with dropsy, ten men with leprosy, the high priest's servant, official's son at Capernaum, sick man, pool of Bethesda, and the man born blind.

So many different situations and so many different methods and styles used by Jesus.

The church down through the ages has either majored on this area of its life, been lukewarm in this area or worst of all, completely ignored it. Today, thankfully, the healing ministry of the Shepherd can be found in most places you look, especially on the streets and in the market place, and you will find many ways that church streams pray for healing, including 'Laying on of hands', 'Anointing with oil', 'Holy water', 'Commanding healing', and 'Praying by His stripes you are healed'. There seems to be no end to the ways the Shepherd would use to heal people. It is His ministry, and we must honour all that He is doing amongst us, whether we understand it or not, and indeed whether it is the 'way' that we do it in our local church system or not.

The Shepherd is asking us to do what He tells us to do, just as He is asking others to do what He tells them to do. We must get away from the idea that 'our way' is the best and only way, and only do what He asks us to do where we are.

As John Wimber memorably said, "We are just small change in His pocket, and He can spend us as He wills."

As a practioner of the Gospel, I have had varying degrees of 'success' (I use this word reluctantly) when praying for physical healing. On the first ministry trip that I went on with David and Irene Betts, we were in Germany, and David took the older folks at the conference off to a separate building, and left my friend Clive Laker, me and a worship team to look after the teenagers. At the end of the meeting, we asked those in the hall who needed a healing touch from Jesus, to come forward and be prayed for. To our utter surprise, at least two hundred young people got out of their seats and ran forward for prayer. Amazing things happened in that hall on that day. It seems like anything we prayed for was answered.

Too many to mention here, but after the meeting, I was having lunch with some of the older teenagers, and through an interpreter, it became clear that one young woman was in deep despair. On the basis that we would not pray for someone of the opposite sex, I asked Irene Betts to come and pray. The problem that the young woman was having, was that she continually suffered from severe stomach pains, and had done since her early teenage years. Through a 'Word of Knowledge' from the Shepherd, Irene 'knew' that the young woman had never had a period in her life. This situation was the complete opposite to the story in the Bible of the 'woman and bleeding', but as Irene spoke out the words that the Shepherd had given her, the young woman got up and rushed out the room crying. Not long later, she came back with a big smile on her face, and although she was still in pain, the Shepherd had healed her.

On another ministry trip, this time to Romania, I was leading a team in a small village, when we were asked to pray for two older ladies. They were both blind from some sort of disease and desperately wanted to see again. After praying, with a female team member, for one of them (to my shame I can't remember her name), her left eye started to change colour from a milky white shade, and her iris started to come clear. Only one of her eyes was healed, but she could see. The other lady remained blind in both eyes, no matter how long we prayed for her.

The next morning, we returned to the same house in the village full of excitement, and on arriving we could see that the healed eye had improved over night, so full of faith, we felt we should pray for the second lady again, trusting God for healing. On asking where the other lady was, we were informed that she had passed away in the night.

I was beginning to fully understand 'the now and not yet' of the Kingdom.

I want to tell you about one other occasion, where the Shepherd was doing His thing, but this time, I need to tell you about the trap of pride that I fell into.

I was leading a ministry team in a village in north west Bulgaria, when one of the villagers came up to us and said that there was a faithful follower of Jesus in the village, who because of her very bad leg problems, had to lean on crutches and hadn't left her house for over three to four months. Could we go and visit her?

Of course, following Mary's instruction, we did what the Shepherd was telling us to do.

After a lengthy prayer time, we sensed that Jesus had done all that He wanted to do, so we thanked the lady for her hospitality and left her home.

Five minutes later, we were walking up the road, when we heard gasps coming from the villagers who were standing outside their homes. Wondering what was going on, we turned around and to our utter surprise, saw the lady we had just prayed for, walking quickly, if not running, without her crutches, trying to catch us up, and in her hands, was an unopened tin of chocolate sweets.

When she reached us, she couldn't stop thanking us for what we had done for her, and then she insisted that we take the tin of chocolate sweets home, to eat and enjoy later.

The lady was overjoyed, the villagers were in a state of shock, and what, may you ask, did I do, other than eat some of the chocolates?

The only answer I can give you is that pride raised its ugly head. Instead of stopping and celebrating the goodness of God, and using the Shepherd's healing as a way of introducing the gospel to the villagers who had seen a miracle in front of their eyes, I said to the lady, "thanks for your kind words and the gift of chocolates", turned around and continued the walk through the village thinking the Kingdom SAS had come to set them free.

My prayer ever since has been for that lady, and that she continued to be blessed by the Shepherd. I also pray that what I did, out of pride, did not interfere with what the Shepherd was doing in that village.

The lesson I have learnt from that day is that you and I don't have a ministry, and therefore it doesn't make sense to be prideful. It is like the often-told story in church about the donkey that carried Jesus in to Jerusalem. When all the people were shouting Hosanna, and making a noise of welcome, the donkey could have been full of pride and saying, "how great I am", with the people agreeing, as they welcomed him in to the city. The reality was, that it was all about Jesus.

All ministry belongs to Jesus, and he graciously calls us to be obedient to His word and then be His hands and feet wherever we find ourselves.

Around the world today, there are wonderful stories of people being healed of all sorts of problems including, but not only, freedom from cancers and tumours, broken bones, heart disease, renewal of limbs, skin diseases, blind eyes, deaf ears, broken knees, and the raising of those who had prematurely died.

Because of the 'now and not yet' of the Kingdom, clearly not everybody who is prayed for is healed, still, the Shepherd calls His followers to pray and do the work of the Kingdom wherever they find themselves, and then leave the outcome of our prayers to Him.

As an encouragement for you to continue praying for the sick, I must mention a couple of vineyard church pastors, who Jo and I planted out into the Medway Towns in Kent.

Andy and Sharon Millar are absolutely committed to praying for the sick wherever and whenever they can. Yes, it is regular in their church services, but more importantly for them, they will pray in the workplace, the shopping centres, coffee shops, the streets, school gates, the street where they live – the list is endless.

Their approach to praying is, I believe, a lesson and instruction from the Shepherd. With a full acknowledgement that until Jesus returns in His glory, not all prayers will be answered here on the earth, that is the 'now and not yet' of the Kingdom, they pray as if they will be answered by the Shepherd, because He has instructed all His followers to do what He did.

I believe the Shepherd is calling all who follow Him today, to be bold and pray more and more for those who are sick amongst you, not just in the meetings of the church but where you live, work and play. On the streets, in the workplace, in the schools and colleges, on public transport, and wherever you find yourselves on a day to day basis. Yes, it might feel daunting, but know that the King of heaven is with you until the end of time.

One thing is certain, if we never pray for the sick, and apart from an intervention from heaven, we will never see what our heart desires in this area of our lives. The Shepherd is calling us to do more for Him, and for those created in His image. People are hurting, and they need a touch from heaven. It is time to stand in the gap for them, and do what we are called to do.

If we believe what we say we believe, we must listen to the Shepherd, and do what He tells us to do.

There will be some who completely disagree with what I am saying, especially those who believe that Jesus doesn't do today what He did when He walked on the earth, and some will argue that when He walked on the earth, Jesus didn't heal everybody who was sick, and undoubtedly this is true. However, Jesus did more than is written in the words that we have before us today, as John confirmed when he said in his gospel:

30 Jesus performed many other signs in the presence of his disciples, which are not recorded in this book. 31 But these are written that you may believe that Jesus is the Messiah, the Son of God, and that by believing you may have life in his name.
(John 20:30-31 NIV)

and

24 This is the disciple who testifies to these things and who wrote them down. We know that his testimony is true.

25 Jesus did many other things as well. If every one of them were written down, I suppose that even the whole world would not have room for the books that would be written.
(John 21:24-25 NIV)

and His instruction to those who follow Him are clear:

Jesus called his twelve disciples to him and gave them authority to drive out impure spirits and to heal every disease and illness. (Matthew 10:1 NIV)

5 These twelve Jesus sent out with the following instructions: 'Do not go among the Gentiles or enter any town of the Samaritans. 6 Go rather to the lost sheep of Israel. 7 As you go, proclaim this message: "The kingdom of heaven has come near." 8 Heal those who are ill, raise the dead, cleanse those who have leprosy, drive out demons. Freely you have received; freely give. (Matthew 10:5-8 NIV)

If you doubt this command is for you, then listen to the Shepherd's words at the end of Matthew's gospel:

18 Then Jesus came to them and said, 'All authority in heaven and on earth has been given to me. 19 Therefore go and make disciples of all nations, baptising them in the name of the Father and of the Son and of the Holy Spirit, 20 and teaching them to obey everything I have commanded you. And surely, I am with you always, to the very end of the age'. (Matthew 28:18-20 NIV)

Now, let's go and do it.

Command over the forces of nature –

Calming the storm, walking on the water, at least 5,000 people fed, at least 4,000 people fed, Coin in the fish's mouth, Fig-tree withered, the catch of fish, water turned into wine, and another catch of fish.

I have seen miraculous provision of food. At the Dartford Church's Food Bank, operated out of the Vineyard church, not once did anybody go away without some provision, and at Christmas times especially, there were wonderful full baskets of food for the whole family.

It's amazing what the Shepherd will do for those who trust Him, and not put their trust in mankind and his schemes.

My wife, Jo and I have many times been the recipients of cash that has dropped through our letter box just when we needed it.

There are far too many stories from people we know, who have had the same happen to them. You almost certainly know at least one person this has happened to?

Regarding the other areas covered under this sub-heading, my many prayers in these have remained unanswered here on the earth. (they certainly have been answered in heaven), but I have been with people whose prayers have calmed stormy seas, stopped major storms and broken the cloud cover with a patch of blue sky the size of a man's hand.

The seventh time the servant reported, 'A cloud as small as a man's hand is rising from the sea'. (1 Kings 18:44 NIV)

Bringing the dead back to life –

Jairus' daughter, Widow's son at Nain, and Lazarus.

I don't have any personal stories to add here, but around the world, if you would only listen, you will hear that this is indeed happening today. Wonderful.

All these amazing miracles are signs that the Kingdom of Heaven has come down to earth, proclaiming the very thing that Isaiah prophesied about the Messiah over 700 years before the birth of Jesus:

1 The Spirit of the Sovereign Lord is on me,
because the Lord has anointed me
to proclaim good news to the poor.
He has sent me to bind up the broken-hearted,
to proclaim freedom for the captives
and release from darkness for the prisoners,
2 to proclaim the year of the Lord's favour
and the day of vengeance of our God,
to comfort all who mourn,
3 and provide for those who grieve in Zion—
to bestow on them a crown of beauty instead of ashes,
the oil of joy instead of mourning,
and a garment of praise instead of a spirit of despair.
(Isaiah 61:1-3 NIV)

Whatever the Shepherd did, and however He did it, over two thousand years ago, can be looked at as a model and a prophetic promise for you and me to follow today.

If the Shepherd has done it before, He will do it again. We only need to have ears that hear what He is saying and then do what He asks us to do.

Second, His mission and purpose:

For I have come down from heaven not to do my will but to do the will of him who sent me. (John 6:38 NIV)

Then I said, 'Here I am—it is written about me in the scroll—I have come to do your will, my God.' (Hebrews 10:7 NIV)

Unlike probably everybody else who ever lived, these verses show that Jesus had no independent agenda. It wasn't about Him; His sole purpose on earth was to do His Father's will.

Today, the Shepherd is about His Father's business, and He is calling all His followers to join in the work.

Third, His prayer life focused completely on His Father:

This, then, is how you should pray:

'Our Father in heaven,

hallowed be your name'. (Matthew 6:9 NIV)

There have been some wonderful instructive books, CDs and DVDs published on the Lord's Prayer, and sermon after sermon which reveal the Shepherd's heart on prayer much better than I could ever do. The only point I believe the Shepherd wants me to make to the reader, is *'PLEASE NEVER STOP PRAYING'.* Every prayer that has ever been prayed or will be prayed in the future, has and will always be, answered by the Father as an immediate response to the prayer. We may not receive the answer straight away in our time, but it has and will be answered. It is the Father's delight to do this for His children.

Do not let the enemy of all mankind rob you of knowing this. By thinking that our prayers sometimes seem to hit a ceiling, and therefore not get through to the throne room, is the surest way of praying less and less.

Fourthly, the cup of suffering in Gethsemane was His Father's cup:

Jesus commanded Peter, 'Put your sword away! Shall I not drink the cup the Father has given me?' (John 18:11 NIV)

I confess that I don't really know too much about this statement, other than the journey that the Shepherd was on was not His own but that which the Father had appointed Him to do.

I believe the cup is meant to signify the wrath of God, and the punishment due to sin, which was endured by Christ in His suffering for all mankind. It was given to Jesus by his Father; because it was The Father who called His son Jesus to this suffering, all because it was appointed and determined by the Father, since sin first entered the world.

Finally, and most importantly of all, the reason for Christ's death & resurrection was so God the Father could bring all of us back to Himself, which is why Jesus said:

I am the way and the truth and the life. No one comes to the Father except through me. (John 14:6 NIV)

And then why Paul reiterates in his second letter to the people of Corinth:

18 All this is from God, who reconciled us to himself through Christ and gave us the ministry of reconciliation: 19 that God was reconciling the world to himself in Christ, not counting people's sins against them. And he has committed to us the message of reconciliation. (2 Corinthians 5:18-19 NIV)

It seems clear to me that the reason Jesus said this, and Paul reiterates it, is because the Shepherd is clearly 'one with the Father' (He and the Father are one) and therefore it is only through Him that we find the way back to the Father both for us and for all mankind.

Throughout the letters ('the epistles') of the New Testament, we can see the writers proclaiming near the beginning of each one, that 'Jesus and the Father are one'.

To all in Rome who are loved by God and called to be his holy people: Grace and peace to you from God our Father and from the Lord Jesus Christ. (Romans 1:7 NIV)

2 To the church of God in Corinth, to those sanctified in Christ Jesus and called to be his holy people, together with all those everywhere who call on the name of our Lord Jesus Christ – their Lord and ours: 3 Grace and peace to you from God our Father and the Lord Jesus Christ. (1 Corinthians 1:2-3 NIV)

3 Grace and peace to you from God our Father and the Lord Jesus Christ, 4 who gave himself for our sins to rescue us from the present evil age, according to the will of our God and Father. (Galatians 1:3-4 NIV)

1 To God's holy people in Ephesus, the faithful in Christ Jesus: 2 Grace and peace to you from God our Father and the Lord Jesus Christ. (Ephesians 1:1-2 NIV)

1 To all God's holy people in Christ Jesus at Philippi, together with the overseers and deacons: 2 Grace and peace to you from God our Father and the Lord Jesus Christ. (Philippians 1:1-2 NIV)

We always thank God, the Father of our Lord Jesus Christ, when we pray for you. (Colossians 1:3 NIV)

Grace and peace to you from God the Father and the Lord Jesus Christ. (2 Thessalonians 1:2 NIV)

To Timothy my true son in the faith: Grace, mercy and peace from God the Father and Christ Jesus our Lord. (1 Timothy 1:2 NIV)

To Titus, my true son in our common faith: Grace and peace from God the Father and Christ Jesus our Saviour. (Titus 1:4 NIV)

1 To Philemon our dear friend and fellow worker – 2 also to Apphia our sister and Archippus our fellow soldier – and to the church that meets in your home:3 Grace and peace to you from God our Father and the Lord Jesus Christ. (Philemon 1;1-3 NIV)

From scripture, we can clearly see God the Father placed right in the centre of the life and ministry of the Shepherd, and therefore, we have to say, right at the centre of the Gospel.

Our relationship with God as our Father needs to be as important to us as Jesus' own relationship was with His Father.

We proclaim to you what we have seen and heard, so that you also may have fellowship with us. And our fellowship is with the Father and with his Son, Jesus Christ. (1 John 1:3 NIV)

The goal of every follower of the Shepherd is to be like Jesus. Being like Jesus is having the same kind of relationship that He has with His Father.

This is the Father's intention for us as who are His sons & daughters.

I somehow came across a quote from a man named Andrew Murray, who was a preacher and writer, and lived between 1828 and 1917, who is reported to have said: *"Jesus' life of dependency on the Father was a life lived in the Father's love. What the Father's love is to Jesus His (the Father's) love will be to us"*

I wish that I had said it!

I have fond memories of the Toronto church conference that I attended, which was titled 'The Father Loves You'. On one of the days, I spent two hours on the floor of the prayer room, weeping my heart out as a worship leader prophetically played and sang his music over me. I have never been closer to my Father than I was on that day and for those two hours. (I am so looking forward to getting back to that place with my Father!)

I am convinced that right now, the Shepherd is saying to all who would listen, "The Father Loves You."

As can be seen from the above, the Father is clearly at the centre of the gospel.

This 'gospel of grace' is all about the Father's love, and Him reaching out in love to His children, who are His by creation, but because of sin are separated from Him. Because of His great love, the Father's wants to embrace His children and through redemption, bring them back into a loving relationship with Himself.

The Gospel is about the Father, who because of His great love, sent His son, Jesus, to be the Saviour of the world.

For God so loved the world that he gave his one and only Son, that whoever believes in him shall not perish but have eternal life. (John 3:16 NIV)

The Gospel is about the obedience of the Son who because of His great love for His Father, obediently came to earth, and died on the cross.

For I have come down from heaven not to do my will but to do the will of him who sent me. (John 6:38 NIV)

And being found in appearance as a man, he humbled himself by becoming obedient to death – even death on a cross! (Philippians 2:8 NIV)

The love of the Son, Jesus, has expressed itself in obedience to the Father.

The Shepherd makes this very clear when He says:

If you knew me, you would know my Father also. (John 8:19 NIV)

Then He put it even stronger when He later says:

If you really know me, you will know my Father as well. From now on, you do know him and have seen him. (John 14:7 NIV)

I hope that you can see from this short study of the Shepherd and the Father, that there are no independent actions between the two, and that the Father is central to all that the Son does.

The Shepherd is directing all who would listen, back to their heavenly Father, for it is the Sons one desire, to see us in the same deep relationship with the Father that He has with His Father.

Questions:

1) Do you know deep down in your heart, that 'The Father Loves You'?

2) Do you come alive when you pray to your heavenly Father?

If the answer to either of these questions is no, then please ask the Shepherd to once again reveal the Father's heart to you, hear what He has to say and do what He tells you to do.

CHAPTER 10

THE SHEPHERD AND THE HOLY SPIRIT

The first person we need to look at before we consider the relationship between the Shepherd and the Holy Spirit, is the Holy Spirit Himself.

The Holy Spirit is an integral part of the Trinity, and therefore shares the same fullness of deity as the Father and the Son (the Shepherd).

When we look at the Holy Spirit, particularly in relation to the Shepherd, we must keep at the forefront of our minds, the essential deity of the Spirit: that is that the Spirit is equal to the Son and not inferior to the Son: He is no less God, He is no less personal, He is no less powerful. He is of the same essence or, if you like, nature as the Father and the Son.

Whilst insisting on the unity and equality of the Spirit and the Son, we must ensure that we don't lose the biblical distinction between the Spirit and the Son in terms of their respective roles, both in heaven and here on the earth.

The Holy Spirit was there with the Father and Son at creation, revealed in Genesis 1:2. He was there overshadowing Jesus' conception recorded in Luke 1:35. He was there at Jesus' baptism seen in Luke 3:22. And He was there at Jesus' temptation finally shown in Luke 4:1-2.

We also see that Jesus performed his miracles through the power of the Spirit, reflecting Isaiah's wonderful prophecy as recorded in Luke 4:14-19.

In the last week of Jesus' earthly life, His close friends betray Him, deny Him, and leave Him. But the Holy Spirit walked with him all the way into the last stronghold of the enemy, that is death, giving Him all the power and strength He needed to offer himself up, for all mankind, freely. You can read about this in Hebrews 9:14.

In Romans 1:4, we can clearly see the relationship between the Shepherd and the Holy Spirit. The Holy Spirit was there in the tomb on Easter Sunday to raise Jesus in the power of the resurrection.

To help us understand the unity and equality between the Son and the Spirit, it is helpful to remember that the Holy Spirit is called 'the Spirit of Christ'. The Holy Spirit is just as much the Spirit of Jesus as he is the Spirit of God. Consider the following verses of scripture:

You, however, are not in the realm of the flesh but are in the realm of the Spirit, if indeed the Spirit of God lives in you. And if anyone does not have the Spirit of Christ, they do not belong to Christ.
(Romans 8:9 NIV)

Because you are his sons, God sent the Spirit of his Son into our hearts, the Spirit who calls out, 'Abba, Father'.
(Galatians 4:6 NIV)

For I know that through your prayers and God's provision of the Spirit of Jesus Christ what has happened to me will turn out for my deliverance.
(Philippians 1:19 NIV)

Trying to find out the time and circumstances to which the Spirit of Christ in them was pointing when he predicted the sufferings of the Messiah and the glories that would follow.
(1Peter 1:11 NIV)

The knowledge that the Holy Spirit is the Spirit of Jesus Christ, should enable us to see that He doesn't work in the arena of the mystical and mysterious, but in the realm of practical, knowable reality. Jesus Christ is the one who became flesh and lived among us: we know what He is like, we saw Him, heard Him, touched Him. We felt His compassion, we saw His power; we were there when He died on the cross, and we witnessed His resurrection by which He secured our salvation and that of all creation. When we speak of the Holy Spirit, it is His Spirit of whom we are speaking, not some unknown and unknowable God, nor some mysterious power.

I heard recently, one preacher who insisted that the Holy Spirit is not weird or odd. People's reaction to Him and what He does may seem weird or odd, but The Holy Spirit Himself is God and God is not weird. I couldn't agree more.

The Holy Spirit is the Spirit of the Shepherd who is our Brother, our Friend, our Saviour, the Spirit of the One who so loved us that he put aside His glory and made himself nothing for our sake and for our eternal life with our Father.

When Jesus told His disciples that the Holy Spirit would come to them, He called the Holy Spirit 'another Counsellor' or in the NIV translation, 'another Advocate'.

And I will ask the Father, and he will give you another advocate to help you and be with you for ever.
(John 14:16 NIV)

The important word in this passage is:

'Another' – 'Allos' (Greek)

Strongs #243

'Another of the same kind; another of a similar type'.

The Shepherd is not promising somebody or something completely different from Himself. He is promising them, and by lineage, us, 'all' that is in God.

This is confirmed when later, the Shepherd, in promising the coming of the Spirit, spoke of that coming as He, Himself coming to the believer:

18 I will not leave you as orphans; I will come to you. 19 Before long, the world will not see me anymore, but you will see me. Because I live, you also will live. 20 On that day you will realise that I am in my Father, and you are in me, and I am in you. 21 Whoever has my commands and keeps them is the one who loves me. The one who loves me will be loved by my Father, and I too will love them and show myself to them.'

22 Then Judas (not Judas Iscariot) said, 'But, Lord, why do you intend to show yourself to us and not to the world?'

23 Jesus replied, 'Anyone who loves me will obey my teaching. My Father will love them, and we will come to them and make our home with them.
(John 14:18-23 NIV)

We must be clear and unequivocal here. Because the Holy Spirit is the Spirit of Jesus, we must not attribute to the Holy Spirit anything that conflicts with the truth about Jesus Christ. The truth of heaven is that the Holy Spirit and Jesus are not rivals, nor do they contradict each other, and they do not, and will not, vie for our allegiance or offer us conflicting or differing blessings.

Jesus says of the Spirit, He will tell you about me and He will bring glory to Me by taking from what is Mine and making it known to you.

But the Advocate, the Holy Spirit, whom the Father will send in my name, will teach you all things and will remind you of everything I have said to you.
(John 14:26 NIV)

14 He will glorify me because it is from me that he will receive what he will make known to you. 15 All that belongs to the Father is mine. That is why I said the Spirit will receive from me what he will make known to you.
(John 16:14,15 NIV)

As one reward for the successful completion of His mission, the Shepherd gave the Holy Spirit and poured Him out on His followers to empower them to continue to finish the task that He had begun. We must view the pouring out of the Holy Spirit as part of the Shepherd's work, just like His teaching and His miracles and His atoning death and His resurrection and His ascension. We could see this as the climax of all He came to do. It is what all the rest was for. Just as the Spirit came down upon Jesus' physical body at His baptism in the River Jordan, now the Shepherd pours the Spirit down upon His followers at Pentecost. What happened to Jesus at His baptism in the River Jordan, is now released at Pentecost for all followers of the Shepherd for all time.

The Holy Spirit's role is to glorify and confirm Jesus to His people.

13 But when he, the Spirit of truth, comes, he will guide you into all the truth. He will not speak on his own; he will speak only what he hears, and he will tell you what is yet to come. 14 He will glorify me because it is from me that he will receive what he will make known to you.
(John 16:13-14 NIV)

The theologian, J I Packer, calls this the Holy Spirit's "floodlight ministry."

The Holy Spirit's distinctive new covenant role, then, is to fulfil what we may call a floodlight ministry in relation to the Lord Jesus Christ. So far as this role was concerned, the Spirit "was not yet" (John 7:39, literal Greek) while Jesus was on earth; only when the Father had glorified him (see John 17:1, 5) could the Spirit's work of making men aware of Jesus' glory begin.

I remember walking to a church one winter evening to preach on the words "he shall glorify me," seeing the building floodlit as I turned a corner, and realizing that this was exactly the illustration my message needed.

When floodlighting is well done, the floodlights are so placed that you do not see them; you are not in fact supposed to see where the light is coming from; what you are meant to see is just the building on which the floodlights are trained. The intended effect is to make it visible when otherwise it would not be seen for the darkness, and to maximize its dignity by throwing all its details into relief so that you see it properly. This perfectly illustrates the Spirit's new covenant role. He is, so to speak, the hidden floodlight shining on the Saviour.

Or think of it this way. It is as if the Spirit stands behind us, throwing light over our shoulder, on Jesus, who stands facing us.

The Spirit's message is never,

"Look at Me; listen to Me; come to Me; get to know Me,"

but always,

"Look at Him, and see His glory; listen to Him, and hear His word; go to Him, and have life; get to know Him, and taste His gift of joy and peace."

('Keeping in Step with the Spirit: Finding Fullness in Our Walk with God' – J I Packer) (11)

If you like, you could say that the second 'comforter/advocate' the Holy Spirit, leads us continually to the original 'comforter/advocate' Jesus.

They cannot be separated. I love the way that Wm Paul Young portrays them in his novel, 'The Shack'. Such a clear understanding of their preference for one another.

Today, the Shepherd is continually guiding new followers to the Holy Spirit. As an example of this work, one does not need to look further than the wonderful worldwide 'Alpha Course'.? The Holy Spirit weekend is amazing. I recommend it to anyone wishing to introduce their family, friends and work colleagues to Jesus.

There is nothing better than being in the company of Holy Spirit filled followers of the Shepherd, who are deeply in love with their heavenly Father.

Questions:

1) Do you know the Holy Spirit, and do you understand what the Holy Spirit is doing in your life?

2) Do you come 'alive' as you respond to the Holy Spirit? If not, why do you think this might be?

3) If you don't know the Holy Spirit as the comforter promised by the Shepherd, why don't you ask Jesus to introduce Him to you? It is His great pleasure to do that for all who ask Him.

CHAPTER 11
THE SHEPHERD AND HIS KINGDOM

Arguably, this could be the most important chapter of them all. It was the last one to be written, and if you like, it could be considered as an afterthought. Once I got my head around the seriousness of the subject, the realisation once again, that my entire Christian life of following the Shepherd has been to help further His Kingdom, why would He not want me to write about it?

I have said at the beginning of this book that, "I must declare that I am deeply in love with Jesus, and passionately sold out for the Kingdom of God". The following is my understanding, as limited as it is, of the Shepherd and His Kingdom.

I need to reiterate again that I am writing this as a practioner, and not a theologian.

It wasn't long after Jo and I planted the Vineyard church in Dartford, that a wonderful young Christian man took me to one side and asked the question, "What do you mean when you keep talking about the Kingdom of God?" I realised at that point that we humans very quickly revert to shorthand in the way we discuss matters, and more worryingly, using either jargon or abbreviations. (Have you ever talked to your family, friends or work colleagues about your faith, and included in the conversations such terms as 'NIV', 'Trinity', 'Small Group', etc.?)

The first thing we need to do, is to describe the Kingdom of God, in the easiest possible terms. I am indebted to John Wimber for this description: 'The Kingdom is primarily a realm over which a king exercises authority'. On this basis, when you read through the Bible you will see that the 'Kingdom of God' is the place where Jesus is King. Everywhere you see the Shepherd proclaiming the Kingdom, manifesting the Kingdom and teaching the people about the Kingdom, you will see the enormity of God 's effective will, revealed.

The Kingdom of God, was, is and always will be, the central message that the Shepherd proclaimed and demonstrated in His life here on the earth. Since Pentecost and throughout the years leading up to today, the Holy Spirit has been activating people to do the works of Jesus in their generation.

When looking in detail at the Kingdom of God, as a Kingdom student and follower myself, I think that like all good teachers, we should try and divide the subject into four sub-sections. These would be:

1) The proclamation of the Kingdom.
2) The parables of the Kingdom.
3) The promise of the Kingdom
4) The power of the Kingdom.

As a start: **_Proclamation._**

It is clear from the Bible that whenever the Kingdom of God is proclaimed, the power of that Kingdom is released. Paul declared in 1 Corinthians 4:20 **"for the Kingdom of God is not in word but in power"**. (NIV) For you and me, this is good news, for as I have written elsewhere in this book, which of us can heal anybody or raise them from the dead?

I believe that John Wimber coined the phrase, 'Power Evangelism', but I may be wrong! However, no matter who did, when you read about the things that the Shepherd did in His earthly time, those amazing three years, it is crystal clear that when He proclaimed the

Gospel, power encounters took place, and more and more people started following Him. The same with His disciples after His death and resurrection. Proclamation, followed by power encounters followed by mass conversion.

My own approach to such proclamations has always been a positive one. As a local church leader, I saw my job as that of seeing what the Shepherd was doing in our fellowship, and then seeking to get behind it, encourage the person who God had been leading in whatever direction He wanted us to go, and then releasing it.

There are two outstanding memories that I have in this matter.

The first happened early in the church plant life. We were quite small in numbers at the time, when one of the ladies in the church felt that we should start a street café to bless the people in the town. There is a small public area around the corner from the church centre, and we felt that it would be a good place to test God's call, as we could fill up hot water containers without too much hassle. It was decided that we would provide the café on Saturday mornings, and as the location was between a car park and the shopping areas, it was felt that this would give us the best chance of 'success'.

Everything went well, and we met a lot of people that we would not have, if we had just stayed in the church centre and served from there. It just went well, but something didn't quite seem right. After further prayer, we decided that we would offer to pray for people on the street, which at the time, freaked out a lot of the helpers working in the street café.

The memory I have comes from about six weeks into the project. We were doing what we normally did when a young man in a wheelchair stopped for a cup of coffee. The team offered to pray for the young man, but he was not interested, and therefore we just served him, talked to him, I can't remember what about, and went about the business of the Kingdom. At the end of two hours after everybody, but the young man, had left to get on with their day, we started to clear up around the young man. To our surprise, he didn't move once, not even after everything had been cleared away. What to do?

Two or three of us started talking to the young man, asking him why he wasn't moving. His response amazed us. Remember that since he had arrived, he hadn't wanted prayer. The young man said that for years he had been in constant pain, turmoil and restlessness, asking questions like, "What is the point of going on?", "Why can't the doctors help me?", and, "How can I sleep without sleeping pills?". He carried on talking, saying that the reason he wasn't moving from the spot he was on, was because he had no pain and he felt peaceful. We never prayed for him, and there was no sign that he had responded to Jesus, but clearly our proclamation of the Kingdom of God on the street that day, resulted in a power encounter for the young man.

I have prayed regularly for that young man, especially that he would remember that day and the people who served him on the street.

The second memory I have is when two of our young women came to Jo and me to talk about a food bank for Dartford.

In partnership with most of the church denominations in the town, we set-up the food bank in the Vineyard Centre, for the people of Dartford.

Success is the wrong word to use for food banks, but success with the people, is absolutely the right outcome for what we do for them in Jesus' name. Alongside the food bank we provided a small selection of food and drinks, and after about eighteen months, it was felt that we should offer prayer alongside everything else we were doing. I can't remember how many people were healed, although it was quite a few, and there was much rejoicing in the team. My memory is about one lady who always seemed to question why we were doing what we were doing, but after a period, and after a small measure of healing in her body, this lovely lady responded to an invitation by one of the team members to come to a church meeting on the following Sunday morning. It wasn't long before she started following the Shepherd, and then her daughter came to faith, and finally her husband followed in their footsteps. It was our privilege to baptise both mother and daughter in the local swimming pool.

Can you see what happens when we follow the commands of the Shepherd to proclaim the Kingdom of God, and in the power of the Holy Spirit, do what He tells us to do?

Next: _Parables._

What do the parables say about Jesus Kingdom?

There are six parables that Jesus tells, which reveal the present reality of The Kingdom of God. These six reveal The Kingdom which Jesus had come out of heaven to bring.

The parable of the sower. (Matthew 13:1-9)

In ancient Palestine, I believe that ploughing came after sowing. This makes sense to me, even as a town dweller, otherwise how would the seed end up in the ground?

If this is the case, then I believe the parable is identifying a truth, which is that we should pay less attention to the type of soil, and major on the act of sowing itself. I remember well, David Ruis, a Vineyard Pastor, teaching on this parable. He said that very often, we followers of the Shepherd think that the seed He has given us to sow, is finite, and that we should sow it sparingly. His teaching was clear and to the point – the seed is plentiful, and we should sow it abundantly. That's our job as disciples. (More on disciples later.)

What is this parable saying about the Kingdom of God? I believe that it represents the reality that the Kingdom of God is breaking into the world, just like the seed is breaking into the ground. The Shepherd is declaring that in Him, the Kingdom has come and that the Rule of God is here.

The parable of the mustard seed. (Matthew 13:31-32)

Here we see the concept of the 'Now and not yet' revealed.

The parable shows the contrast between the present and future reality of the Kingdom. In the parable there is a small mustard seed and a large bush or tree. We know that a seed has everything within itself to birth and grow a bush or tree to maturity, and likewise, Jesus is telling His followers that in His presence, they are tasting what the Kingdom will be like in its fulness.

Oh, how we long for that day!

The parable of the leaven. (Matthew 13:33)

Probably like many of you, I have heard so many sermons on the leaven in this parable, so I think the best way I can summarise it is by stating the obvious.

The parable is talking about the transforming power of the Gospel. The Kingdom of God has within itself, the power to transform all of creation, the society we live in, and our own personal lives and circumstances.

The parable of the treasure. (Matthew 13:44)

This parable, like the following one, is all about value. The Kingdom of God, and being a subject of it, is beyond comparison with anything else. There is nothing in this world that we might strive after, that compares with it.

We can spend all our time in amassing wealth, but when we die, it is all lost to us. We cannot take it with us where we are going.

The parable talks about a man who stumbles on the Kingdom of God without looking for it. When the man finds it, he discovers that it is worth more than anything that he has amassed in his life. He knew.

Unlike the rich young ruler, we read about in Luke 18, this man knew what he must do, so he sells all that he owns to purchase the treasure.

The parable of the fine pearls. (Matthew 13:45-46)

This parable is identical in its teaching to the previous one. The main difference being that the person who finds the 'Pearl of great price', was actively seeking the Kingdom, and finds it.

In both these parables, the Shepherd says to those who would follow Him and receive the Kingdom, to leave everything that they have valued in the past behind, and come.

The parable of the net. (Matthew 13:47-50)

This final parable is about judgement and separation.

The first five parables are really talking about the present reality. If you like, the 'Now' in the 'Now and not yet'. This parable is revealing the future reality of the Kingdom of God. In this future, promised by the parable, there will be a complete and perfect community, where the King of Heaven will rule and reign with justice and mercy, where tears and strife will be washed away, and where those who do not belong are separated from those who do.

At the end of this last parable, Jesus asks His followers one simple question. "Have you understood all these things?"

It is a good question for you and me too.

Next: ___Promise.___

The promised future Kingdom invaded the present, in the form of a small baby wrapped in baby clothes and lying in a manger. Sad to say that some people still see the King of Heaven in that state, yet if they would only open their heart, they will see with their mind's eye, that this baby came to change everything.

Around thirty years after this baby's birth, we hear Jesus say,

"The kingdom of God has come near. Repent and believe the good news!"

The absolute truth is, that with Jesus' birth, life, death, and resurrection, the promised Kingdom of God has been established in the world, but it is not yet here in its fulness.

This future Kingdom has already been inaugurated. In the mighty resurrection of Jesus, God has abolished death and has, for all who have eyes to see, shown the whole of creation, the life of the Age to come.

For those who follow the Shepherd, they live the life of the new age now. If you say, as Paul said, "I am in Christ", then you are saying to the world that you are already experiencing the life and power of the promised age to come. Although real, this experience of the future Kingdom is only partial, and it can only be so. The fulness of the Kingdom requires this present age to give way, where everything mortal is 'swallowed up', as Paul says in 2 Corinthians 5:4.

So as mentioned at the beginning of this segment, Jesus came to earth as a baby, to change everything. To fully bring about the change, that is the age to come, Jesus must return to complete the work He has already begun. Oh, how we keep repeating, **"Even so, come Lord Jesus"**.

As we declare regularly in Vineyard churches around the world, "We believe that God's kingdom has come in the ministry of our Lord Jesus Christ, that it continues to come in the ministry of the Spirit through the Church, and that it will be consummated in the glorious, visible, and triumphant appearing of Christ – His return to the earth as King. After Christ returns to reign, He will bring about the final defeat of Satan and all his minions and works, the resurrection of the dead, the final judgment and the eternal blessing of the righteous, and eternal conscious punishment of the wicked. Finally, God will be all in all and His kingdom, His rule and reign, will be fulfilled in the new heavens and the new earth, recreated by His mighty power, in which righteousness dwells and in which He will forever be worshipped".

Finally: *Power.*

The power of the Kingdom must be combined with authority. Jesus made a promise to all who would follow Him, that it would be He that would give such power and authority. I paraphrase what Jesus said to Peter in Matthew 16:18: "The gates of Hell will not be able to withstand the advancing church".

What the Shepherd is saying is that it is His job to build His church. His church will go forward to reclaim those who have been stolen from Him by the enemy, and the enemy's stronghold gates will not be able to stop the church's advance.

The Bible says that He who is in us is greater than he who is in the world. What can this mean? It must be that Jesus' power is greater than the power of His enemy. This statement looks like a train crash waiting to happen. As some preacher once said, "when there is a head-on conflict between the power of the enemy and the power of God, the power of the enemy will lose every time".

Have you got the revelation of this heavenly power yet? Paul prayed in Ephesians 1:19 that we would begin to understand the incredible greatness of the power of God.

It is not only an understanding that we need, although that is essential, it is being clothed with it before we can do what He tells us to do. Right between Jesus' resurrection and ascension to His Father, he exhorts His followers several times about His commission for them to go through Jerusalem, Judea, Samaria, and the uttermost parts of the earth. He told them not to even think of starting on this mission, until they were first clothed with power from His Father on high.

The followers of the Shepherd do exactly what we should do. They wait. For them it was in the upper room where they used to hide after

Ron Warren

the crucifixion. It was in this same room that God's Spirit was released upon them, and they were clothed with power.

According to Jesus, His church is to carry on the ministry that He began over 2,000 years ago, all as recorded in the Bible. His instructions are clear and unequivocal. 'As the Father has sent me, I am sending you'. This instruction was to His followers at the end of His earthly ministry. He's saying I'm now sending you out the same way the Father sent me out. As for His followers back then, so to His followers today.

How about the words of Paul in Ephesians 1?

The power that God has released in us is the same as the mighty strength He exerted when He raised Jesus from the dead. Not only that, but He has seated Him at His right hand in the heavenly realms.

A question for us again. How many of us even think, let alone know, that our bodies, that is our very being, carry the power of God? The same power that raised Jesus from death.

Yet, another question. How many of us ask, 'If this is true, do I need more power?' If this is your question, I can tell you that the answer is simple yet profound. If you are a follower of the Shepherd, you have all the power you will ever need. Remember, it is the same power, not a different one or a fragment of the real one, that raised Jesus from the dead.

We don't need more power. What we need is a release of the power that God has already given to us in our followership of Jesus through His salvation, together with the infilling of the Holy Spirit.

Finally, what could possibly limit the release of this heavenly power in my life? The answer to this question can be seen at the beginning of this segment. "It would be Jesus that would give such power and authority".

It seems clear to me that it is fraudulent to try and minister under God's authority when we are not living under that authority ourselves. As we read the New Testament, we can see that Jesus was true God and yet lived as true man, living under His Father's authority.

Jesus classic statement was, 'I only do what I see the Father doing'. Jesus is saying that He lived and ministered under the authority of His Heavenly Father. If you want to minister in power, stay close to your heavenly Father, keep on being filled with the Holy Spirit, and as His mother Mary said, "do whatever He tells you to do".

Questions:

1) How does it feel to know that Jesus promise of the Kingdom, is a real promise? In the truth of that, how would you change the way you live your life today, if at all?

2) How do you respond to the four statements, 'the proclamation of the Kingdom, parables of the Kingdom, promise of the Kingdom and power of the Kingdom'? Can you put it into your own words?

CHAPTER 12
THE SHEPHERD
BEFORE THE CROSS

The story of the final hours of the Shepherd, before He went to His cross, starts after He and His followers had eaten, what we usually call today the Last Supper.

We read in Matthew's gospel:

36 Then Jesus went with his disciples to a place called Gethsemane, and he said to them, 'Sit here while I go over there and pray.' 37 He took Peter and the two sons of Zebedee along with him, and he began to be sorrowful and troubled. 38 Then he said to them, 'My soul is overwhelmed with sorrow to the point of death. Stay here and keep watch with me.'

39 Going a little farther, he fell with his face to the ground and prayed, 'My Father, if it is possible, may this cup be taken from me. Yet not as I will, but as you will.'

40 Then he returned to his disciples and found them sleeping. 'Couldn't you men keep watch with me for one hour?' he asked Peter. 41 'Watch and pray so that you will not fall into temptation. The spirit is willing, but the flesh is weak.'

42 He went away a second time and prayed, 'My Father, if it is not possible for this cup to be taken away unless I drink it, may your will be done.'

43 When he came back, he again found them sleeping, because their eyes were heavy. 44 So he left them and went away once more and prayed the third time, saying the same thing.

45 Then he returned to the disciples and said to them, 'Are you still sleeping and resting? Look, the hour has come, and the Son of Man is delivered into the hands of sinners. 46 Rise! Let us go! Here comes my betrayer!'
(Matthew 26:36-46 NIV)

Can you sense the humanness of the Shepherd here? He wants His closest friends around Him as He, full of fear, doubt and sorrow, faces the coming days. Wouldn't you want the same? They obviously couldn't stay awake though, as He had to rouse them three times. I can only conclude, that like myself after a good hearty meal, they were full of food and wine and very drowsy.

The text says that He prayed to His Father three times to be released from what He knew was coming, but each time we see that His only desire was to do the will of His Father, whatever that would mean.

Then the betrayer comes. There is nothing more here for me to say, other than He was betrayed. After this, we are told that, ALL His disciples forsook Him and fled.

The Shepherd is now on His own.

The story continues when the Shepherd faces the Sanhedrin, the Jewish authority. Then He is sent to Pontius Pilate, the Roman Governor. Pilate is warned by his wife not to do anything to Jesus, and he tries to get Him released by telling the Jewish people that he can release one prisoner and then asking the Jewish people who they wanted released?

The choice Pilate gave them was a man named Barabbas, the one that Peter later called a murderer, or Jesus.

You disowned the Holy and Righteous One and asked that a murderer be released to you.
(Acts 3:14 NIV)

It is the Jewish people, urged on by some of the members of the Sanhedrin, who cry out for Barabbas to be freed, and then Jesus to be crucified. So thus, the final scene that will change all of creation, for all time, is set.

The story after this is gruesome, and I confess that when I watched Mel Gibson's film 'Passion of The Christ', I couldn't stop crying, seeing what He must have suffered, which, was probably far more violent than a film maker can portray on a screen through a camera.

Like other subjects in this book, there are many excellent books and sermons published on this subject, and I know that I am unable to add to them in any way.

So, we finally come to what the Shepherd says on His cross, which is what I believe He wants to highlight in this book.

It is His words, whilst suffering for each of us, that we must look at.

There seems to be seven important words recorded in the Bible for us to hear.

The first word is, 'FORGIVE'.

Jesus said, 'Father, forgive them, for they do not know what they are doing.'
(Luke 23:34 NIV)

The Shepherd is looking down from the cross, just after he was placed there between two criminals. He sees the Roman soldiers who in turn have mocked Him, scourged Him, and tortured Him, and who have just hammered the nails through His hands and feet into the wood. He may even have remembered those who have sentenced him - Caiaphas and the high priests of the Sanhedrin and Pilate, the Roman Governor. But a more interesting question is, was Jesus also thinking of his disciples and followers who have deserted him, His friend Peter, who has denied him three times to the fickle crowd, who only days before had shouted out praises to Him when He entered Jerusalem, and then within days, chose the Saviour of the world over Barabbas to be crucified?

What about us? Do you think that He might also be thinking about all of those who are to come in the years leading up to His second coming, who, daily, will forget Him in the busyness of their lives?

How does He react? With anger? No, not at all. At the height of His physical suffering, His wonderful love prevails, as He asks His Father to forgive! Can you see what is happening? Jesus asks His Father to forgive, but the reality is that it is only by His sacrifice on the Cross, that mankind can be forgiven.

Right up to the very end, Jesus is preaching forgiveness.

He teaches forgiveness in the Lord's prayer:

And forgive us our debts, as we also have forgiven our debtors. (Matthew 6:12 NIV)

When asked by Peter, how many times should we forgive someone, Jesus answers:

21 Then Peter came to Jesus and asked, 'Lord, how many times shall I forgive my brother or sister who sins against me? Up to seven times?'

22 Jesus answered, 'I tell you, not seven times, but seventy-seven times.' (Matthew 18:21-22 NIV)

At the Last Supper, Jesus explains His coming crucifixion to His apostles when He tells them to drink of the cup:

27 Then he took a cup, and when he had given thanks, he gave it to them, saying, 'Drink from it, all of you. 28 This is my blood of the covenant, which is poured out for many for the forgiveness of sins.

"Drink of it, all of you; for this is my blood of the covenant, which is poured out for many for the forgiveness of sins".
(Matthew 26:27-28 NIV)

The Shepherd forgives the paralysed man at Capernaum:

When Jesus saw their faith, he said to the paralysed man, 'Son, your sins are forgiven.'
(Mark 2:5 NIV)

When He is confronted with the adulteress who seemingly was caught in the act, and about to be stoned, this is how Jesus responded:

6-8 Jesus bent down and wrote with his finger in the dirt. They kept at him, badgering him. He straightened up and said, "The sinless one among you, go first: Throw the stone." Bending down again, he wrote some more in the dirt.

9-10 Hearing that, they walked away, one after another, beginning with the oldest. The woman was left alone. Jesus stood up and spoke to her. "Woman, where are they? Does no one condemn you?"

11 "No one, Master." "Neither do I," said Jesus. "Go on your way. From now on, don't sin."
(John 8:6-11 The Message)

Even though this follows His Resurrection, the Shepherd's first act is to instruct His disciples on why they should forgive:

22 And with that he breathed on them and said, 'Receive the Holy Spirit. 23 If you forgive anyone's sins, their sins are forgiven; if you do not forgive them, they are not forgiven.'
(John 20:22-23 NIV)

To forgive somebody, releases all the power of heaven in to that person's life. If you have been forgiven yourself by anybody, you will know this truth if you are honest with yourself. Just think how much more freedom is released in you, when you are forgiven by the King of heaven?

The second word is 'LOVE AND MERCY' to the criminal hanging on a cross next to Him.

39 One of the criminals who hung there, hurled insults at him: 'Aren't you the Messiah? Save yourself and us!'

40 But the other criminal rebuked him. 'Don't you fear God,' he said, 'since you are under the same sentence? 41 We are punished justly, for we are getting what our deeds deserve. But this man has done nothing wrong.'

42 Then he said, 'Jesus, remember me when you come into your kingdom.'

43 Jesus answered him, 'Truly I tell you, today you will be with me in paradise.'
(Luke 23:39-43 NIV)

It wasn't just the religious leaders, the Roman Governor, the crowd and the soldiers who mocked Jesus. One of the criminals also joined in. But the criminal on the right speaks up for Jesus, as he explains that the two criminals are receiving all they deserve, whereas he says, '**this man has done nothing wrong**'. Then, turning to Jesus, he asks, **Jesus,** '**remember me when you come in your kingdom**'. What wonderful faith this poor man has in Jesus. Compare the faith of this wretched man with that of 'doubting Thomas', one of the Shepherd's early disciples.

Ignoring his own suffering as He hangs there, which must have been unbearable, Jesus' response to the man is one of love and mercy.

This word is again about forgiveness, this time directing it to a sinner. On the cross, Jesus shows His Divinity to the man next to Him hanging on an adjoining cross, by opening heaven for the repentant sinner, who is suffering the same pain of crucifixion.

Can you see the generosity that the Shepherd is showing to a man, whose only request was to be remembered? The world is full of people who just want to be remembered. Are you one of them?

The third word is to His mother, Mary.

25 Near the cross of Jesus stood his mother, his mother's sister, Mary the wife of Clopas, and Mary Magdalene. 26 When Jesus saw his mother there, and the disciple whom he loved standing nearby, he said to her, 'Woman, here is your son,' 27 and to the disciple, 'Here is your mother.' From that time on, this disciple took her into his home.

"Jesus said to his mother: "Woman, this is your son."

Then he said to the disciple: "This is your mother."
(John 19:25-27 NIV)

I have said previously in this book, that we would talk about this interaction between the Shepherd and His mother in more detail.

Here we find Jesus and Mary together again. At the beginning of his three years of ministry in Cana, we see Jesus and Mary together at the wedding feast, talked about in John 2:1-11. Remember this is when Mary said to the servants, **'whatever He tells you to do, do it'.**

This is the recurring theme of this book.

Now we find Mary, at the end of the Shepherd's public ministry, at the foot of His cross.

How can we possibly know what sorrow fills Mary's heart?

I have spoken to many mothers whose children have died before them, and their grief is unending. It is not supposed to happen. Our children are supposed to outlive us. That is the way it is supposed to be. I can't imagine what it must be like for parents, whose children die in combat, fighting for their country. It is just a horrendous thought for me.

What must it have been like for Mary to see her Son mocked, tortured, and crucified? A sword pierces Mary's soul as we are reminded of the prediction given by Simeon at the Temple:

33 The child's father and mother marvelled at what was said about him. 34 Then Simeon blessed them and said to Mary, his mother: 'This child is destined to cause the falling and rising of many in Israel, and to be a sign that will be spoken against, 35 so that the thoughts of many hearts will be revealed. And a sword will pierce your own soul too.'
(Luke 2:33-35 NIV)

There are four of the Shepherd's family and friends recorded as being at the foot of the cross. Mary His mother, John, the disciple whom He loved, Mary of Cleopas, who I am told is His mother's sister, and Mary Magdalene. This third word is addressed to His mother Mary and His dear friend John, who we believe, was the only eye-witness to write about all these things.

Jesus rises above His agony and pain, and shows His deep concern for the ones who love Him. We can see here the good son that the Shepherd is, deeply concerned for His mother. The Shepherd knows what is coming, and He knows how it all came about in the beginning for His mother. Visitations by angels, a wedding not as planned, a birth in a stable, visits by shepherds and then Wise Men from the East, exiled into Egypt, and a family life in Nazareth, with her son learning how to become a carpenter. The Shepherd knew. Now He brings His mother and His dear friend together. The Shepherd charges John to 'look after' Mary.

Is it possible for us to understand the miracle that happens in the womb of a woman, when she conceives? One thing we do know for certain, is that our heavenly Father knows. None who have been born, are outside of that knowledge.

The fourth word we hear, is the one the Shepherd speaks to His Father.

45 From noon until three in the afternoon darkness came over all the land. 46 About three in the afternoon Jesus cried out in a loud voice, 'Eli, Eli, lema sabachthani?' (which means 'My God, my God, why have you forsaken me?')
(Matthew 27:45-46 NIV)

33 At noon, darkness came over the whole land until three in the afternoon. 34 And at three in the afternoon Jesus cried out in a loud voice, 'Eloi, Eloi, lema sabachthani?' (which means 'My God, my God, why have you forsaken me?').
(Mark 15:33-34 NIV)

I have mentioned elsewhere in this book, that when something is repeated in the bible, we should take special note of what is being said. It doesn't mean that what is being said is more important than the rest of what is written in the bible, it just means, 'take care of what you are reading'.

Both Matthew and Mark recall that it was in the ninth hour, after three hours of darkness, that Jesus cried out this word to His Father. Mark brings the whole story to a devastating end when he says, **with a loud cry, Jesus breathed his last.** (Mark 15:37 NIV) Mark is saying, "the Shepherd is dead!"

Compare these words to the first three words of Jesus that we have looked at above. These words are undoubtedly a cry of anguish from the heart of the human Jesus. He must have felt deserted by His Father and the Holy Spirit. Jesus has been with them forever, and now they are not there. Jesus feels the same separation from His Father, that all mankind has known since the fall in the Garden of Eden. The Shepherd is now all alone, and He must face death all by Himself.

Here is the reality for you and me. This is exactly what happens to all of us when we die. We too like Jesus, are all alone at the time of death. By dying in this way, Jesus completely lives the human experience as we must, and by doing so, He wonderfully frees us from the clutches of death.

For the followers of the Shepherd at the time of His crucifixion, they surely couldn't have imagined a more dreadful moment in the history of mankind. Jesus, who came to redeem and save all things is crucified. Jesus is about to be engulfed in the overwhelming flood of everyone's sin. Evil appears to triumph, but it is only for the blink of an eye. The burden of all the sins of humanity, for just a moment in time, overwhelm the humanity of the Saviour of the world.

The amazing redemption plan of The Father requires this to happen. It must happen if Jesus is to save us. It is the defeat of Jesus' humanity that allows the Divine plan of His Father to be completed. It is through the death of the Shepherd, that we are redeemed.

4-6 He wants not only us, but everyone saved, you know, everyone to get to know the truth we've learned: that there's one God and only one, and one Priest-Mediator between God and us—Jesus, who offered himself in exchange for everyone held captive by sin, to set them all free.
(1 Timothy 2:4-6 The Message)

21-25 This is the kind of life you've been invited into, the kind of life Christ lived. He suffered everything that came his way so you would know that it could be done, and also know how to do it, step-by-step.

He never did one thing wrong, not once said anything amiss.

They called him every name in the book and he said nothing back. He suffered in silence, content to let God set things right. He used his servant body to carry our sins to the Cross, so we could be rid of

sin, free to live the right way. His wounds became your healing. You were lost sheep with no idea who you were or where you were going. Now you're named and kept for good by the Shepherd of your souls. (1 Peter 2:21-25 The Message)

Can you see it?

The fifth word we hear is very human – "I am thirsty".

28 Later, knowing that everything had now been finished, and so that Scripture would be fulfilled, Jesus said, 'I am thirsty.' 29 A jar of wine vinegar was there, so they soaked a sponge in it, put the sponge on a stalk of the hyssop plant, and lifted it to Jesus' lips. 30 When he had received the drink, Jesus said, 'It is finished.' With that, he bowed his head and gave up his spirit.
(John 19:28-30 NIV)

When you or I are physically ill, the usual command from those who treat us is, "Keep hydrated." There are of course, some exceptions to this rule, but frankly, there aren't that many.

The phrase Jesus is using here could be called His only human expression of His physical suffering. The truth is Jesus must now be in shock. The wounds He suffered in the scourging, the crowning with thorns, losing blood on the long arduous walk through the city of Jerusalem to where His cross stood waiting for Him, and the final nailing into the wood and the lifting of that cross are finally taking their toll.

So, there is a physical thirst.

But that is not all there is. There is another type of thirst that the Shepherd is talking about. There is a thirst in a spiritual sense.

In the Gospel of John, we see this different type of thirst.

6 Jacob's well was there, and Jesus, tired as he was from the journey, sat down by the well. It was about noon.

7 When a Samaritan woman came to draw water, Jesus said to her, 'Will you give me a drink?' 8 (His disciples had gone into the town to buy food.)

9 The Samaritan woman said to him, 'You are a Jew and I am a Samaritan woman. How can you ask me for a drink?' (For Jews do not associate with Samaritans.)

10 Jesus answered her, 'If you knew the gift of God and who it is that asks you for a drink, you would have asked him, and he would have given you living water.'

11 'Sir,' the woman said, 'you have nothing to draw with and the well is deep. Where can you get this living water? 12 Are you greater than our father Jacob, who gave us the well and drank from it himself, as did also his sons and his livestock?'

13 Jesus answered, 'Everyone who drinks this water will be thirsty again, 14 but whoever drinks the water I give them will never thirst. Indeed, the water I give them will become in them a spring of water welling up to eternal life.'
(John 4:1-14 NIV)

The Shepherd is thirsting for love. He thirsts for the love of His Father - oh how He needs Him now – the one He has known and been with for all time, has left him all alone during this awful last moment when He must fulfil His mission without heaven. The Shepherd also thirsts for the love and salvation of His people, the ones made in His image, the ones He knows intimately from their conception in their mother's wombs, the whole human race.

Do you know that the Shepherd thirsts for you right now?

<u>**The sixth and seventh words are different perspectives if you like, of the Shepherd's last words on the cross.**</u>

28 Later, knowing that everything had now been finished, and so that Scripture would be fulfilled, Jesus said, 'I am thirsty.' 29 A jar of wine vinegar was there, so they soaked a sponge in it, put the sponge on a stalk of the hyssop plant, and lifted it to Jesus' lips. 30 When he had received the drink, Jesus said, 'It is finished.' With that, he bowed his head and gave up his spirit.
(John 19:28-30 NIV)

44 It was now about noon, and darkness came over the whole land until three in the afternoon, 45 for the sun stopped shining. And the curtain of the temple was torn in two. 46 Jesus called out with a loud voice, 'Father, into your hands I commit my spirit.' When he had said this, he breathed his last.
(Luke 23:44-46 NIV)

John, in mentioning the phrase 'it is finished', is recalling the sacrifice of the Passover Lamb mentioned in Exodus 12. Paul also notes that:

For Christ, our Passover lamb, has been sacrificed.
(1 Corinthians 5:7 NIV)

The innocent Lamb, that is Jesus of Nazareth, was slain for our sins, so that you and I might be forgiven. This statement of the Shepherd is His recognition that His suffering is now over and the task His Father gave Him is now completed. Jesus is obedient to the Father and shows His love for all mankind by redeeming us with His death on the Cross.

I can't remember who said the following, but I wish it could have been me, 'what was the darkest day of mankind, became the brightest day for mankind'. Brilliant.

Luke, in recording these words of the Shepherd, 'Father, into your hands I commit my spirit,' is showing that they are His last prayer directed to His Father in heaven. Just before He dies, the Shepherd is recalling the words of Psalm 31:

1 In you, Lord, I have taken refuge; let me never be put to shame; deliver me in your righteousness. 2 Turn your ear to me, come quickly to my rescue; be my rock of refuge, a strong fortress to save me. 3 Since you are my rock and my fortress for the sake of your name lead and guide me. 4 Keep me free from the trap that is set for me, for you are my refuge. 5 Into your hands I commit my spirit.
(Psalm 31:1-5 NIV)

The deep and never-ending relationship between Jesus and His Father, is fully revealed in John's gospel account, where he says, 'I and the Father are one' (10:30), and again at the Last Supper: 'Don't you believe that I am in the Father, and that the Father is in me? The words I say to you I do not speak on my own authority. Rather, it is the Father, living in me, who is doing his work'. (14:10). And finally, 'I came from the Father and entered the world; now I am leaving the world and going back to the Father'. (16:28) (All NIV)

The Shepherd has fulfilled His mission, and that of His Father, once and for all time, on the Cross:

For God so loved the world that he gave his one and only Son, that whoever believes in him shall not perish but have eternal life.
(John 3:16 NIV)

Questions:

1) What do you feel when you are on your own or lonely? Maybe you have your closest friends around you, but you are full of fear, doubt or sorrow. How would it feel to know that Jesus promises never to leave you, or forsake you, no matter what you feel or what you might have done?

2) What do the words, 'Forgive', 'Love' and 'Mercy', mean to you? Is it possible that they might reflect the heart of your Saviour and your heavenly Father?

CHAPTER 13

THE RESURRECTED SHEPHERD (LUKE 24:13-35)

IT IS TRUE

This journey with the Shepherd, as recalled in the Bible, is both literal and spiritual. It is about confirming that no matter what people thought, the absolute reality is that everything the Shepherd had said is true.

This is the story of just two of the followers of Jesus, who were maybe husband and wife, who after the crucifixion and resurrection of their Lord, walk approximately seven miles on an unmade and almost certainly dangerous road from Jerusalem, back to presumably their home in the village of Emmaus.

Although clearly these two disciples had known who Jesus was, and they had probably walked miles with Him and His followers before His crucifixion, on this occasion, they did not recognize Him. You might say they knew a lot about Him. They had probably been witnesses to all the things that had happened in Jerusalem. They may even have been around with the other followers of Jesus and heard the things Jesus had testified about Himself. Even so, on this journey, maybe in despair, or just plain blindness, they were unable to recognize Jesus when they met Him.

There could be several reasons why they did not recognize Jesus on this journey:

Maybe the Shepherd did not want them to recognize Him? More likely, these disciples, like all of mankind, were blind to the reality of the true meaning of how God was redeeming everything to Himself.

A theologian friend of mine recently suggested that the story of the man born blind in John 9 shows a key to the blindness of mankind.

1 As he went along, he saw a man blind from birth. 2 His disciples asked him, "Rabbi, who sinned, this man or his parents, that he was born blind?"

3 "Neither this man nor his parents sinned," said Jesus, "but this happened so that the works of God might be displayed in him. 4 As long as it is day, we must do the works of him who sent me. Night is coming, when no one can work. 5 While I am in the world, I am the light of the world."

6 After saying this, he spat on the ground, made some mud with the saliva, and put it on the man's eyes. 7 "Go," he told him, "wash in the Pool of Siloam" (this word means "Sent"). So the man went and washed, and came home seeing.
(John 9:1-6 NIV)

26 Then they asked him, "What did he do to you? How did he open your eyes?"

27 He answered, "I have told you already and you did not listen. Why do you want to hear it again? Do you want to become his disciples too?"

28 Then they hurled insults at him and said, "You are this fellow's disciple! We are disciples of Moses! 29 We know that God spoke to Moses, but as for this fellow, we don't even know where he comes from."

30 The man answered, "Now that is remarkable! You don't know where he comes from, yet he opened my eyes. 31 We know that God does not listen to sinners. He listens to the godly person who does his will. 32 Nobody has ever heard of opening the eyes of a man born blind. 33 If this man were not from God, he could do nothing."

34 To this they replied, "You were steeped in sin at birth; how dare you lecture us!" And they threw him out.

35 Jesus heard that they had thrown him out, and when he found him, he said, "Do you believe in the Son of Man?"

36 "Who is he, sir?" the man asked. "Tell me so that I may believe in him."

37 Jesus said, "You have now seen him; in fact, he is the one speaking with you."

38 Then the man said, "Lord, I believe," and he worshiped him. (John 9:26-41 NIV)

From verses 36 to 38 it can be clearly seen that it is Jesus that brings sight and clarity to people who are blind.

Getting back to the story of the two disciples on the road with Jesus, I can't think that Jesus is being unkind here. Perhaps if this was His doing, His gradual revelation of Himself was to allow them to learn many lessons about trusting God's promises, but as I say, it is more likely the fact that they were blind to what had happened. I leave this thought for those who are much more knowledgeable on these matters.

Whatever the reason, these followers of Jesus had heard about the events leading up to the crucifixion and resurrection many times, but they seemed to have great difficulty in believing with their 'faith eyes' what has exactly happened.

Indeed, the outcome of what happened in Jerusalem was exactly the opposite of what was expected by all of Jesus' followers. They had their own ideas of who Jesus was, of what He had come to do, and in their own minds, how He should do it.

When things did not turn out like they thought they should, it appears they dismissed the whole thing as a failure, and as misplaced hope and trust.

Why did they have such little faith left in their lives?

They must have heard the reports of the women who went to the tomb. They maybe had even seen the empty tomb for themselves. Still they had not believed. The supernatural power of God to raise Jesus from the dead was just outside of their understanding.

The question this raises is, had they ever seriously considered who this Jesus was that they had willingly followed? Just because they knew Jesus the man, as He walked the land, does not mean they really knew Him.

Just because they had seen Him does not mean they could see who He was. Their eyes had not been opened. It seems clear to me that knowing about Him and knowing Him are two completely different things.

Just before the three of them arrived at the home they were returning to, verse 27 in Luke 24 says, **and beginning with Moses and all the Prophets, he explained to them what was said in all the scriptures concerning himself. (NIV)**

The Bible does not say which passages of scripture Jesus used, but it does say that He opened to the two of them the scriptures with the purpose of showing them how all the Old Testament stories pointed to Him as its fulfilment.

The scriptures gave witness to who He was, why He had come, and why it was necessary for Him to willingly go to the cross and suffer both the pain and ignominy of death.

It seems to me that Jesus probably wanted them to see that if they would only believe what the scriptures say about Him, they would understand why He came and why He had to suffer. They would have known who He was.

If we want to be guided by the Shepherd today, we need to see that scripture gives testimony of who Jesus is. If you want to know Him and hear His voice let Him use scripture today to open your eyes.

He said to him, 'If they do not listen to Moses and the Prophets, they will not be convinced even if someone rises from the dead'. (Luke 16:31 NIV)

Philip found Nathanael and told him, "We have found the one Moses wrote about in the Law, and about whom the prophets also wrote—Jesus of Nazareth, the son of Joseph". (John 1:45 NIV)

Many people today, and indeed those who have gone before us, try to define who Jesus was and maybe is. They might even use a phrase something like "Jesus is one of many ways to get to Heaven." They might say He was a good man, or a great prophet, or a good teacher, or even a rebel who defied the Roman authorities. Have you used a phrase like any of these recently?

According to the Shepherd's own voice, outside of a knowledge of scripture we will never have a proper understanding of who He is. When we get to know the scriptures, we find that they will build our faith, and this will enable us to understand that only through faith can we come to Jesus. The truth of scripture about Jesus leads to personal faith in Him.

Maybe the whole reason for this story being in the Bible is to show us that God prevented these two disciples from recognizing Jesus and to reveal a great truth. The truth that even if we were to see, we might still not believe. We must trust the voice of the Shepherd and the testimony of scripture.

It is as true today as it has ever been, outside of the word of God there is no reliable witness to who Jesus really is.

As we read on in the passage, we get to the point where the Shepherd reveals himself.

Look in Luke 24, verses 30 and 31:

When he was at the table with them, he took bread, gave thanks, broke it and began to give it to them. Then their eyes were opened, and they recognized him, and he disappeared from their sight. (NIV)

It was as they sat down and had fellowship with Jesus, that He disclosed Himself to them.

It seems significant to me that it is around the meal table that the disciples' eyes are opened, and they see Jesus for who He really is.

After His resurrection, many of His appearances were associated with food. Look at Luke 24:41-43, Acts 1:4, and in John 21:9-15. In the intimacy of a meal, Jesus revealed Himself to His followers. His working in their lives became clearer to them, His voice became clearer to those who would listen, and His provision and protection were revealed right in front of their eyes.

For us today, participating in the communion meal, that is the breaking of bread and drinking wine, can have the same truths revealed, if we are prepared to listen to His words.

Back to the story. The verse goes on to say that when His followers recognized Him He disappeared.

The question I keep on asking is why?

In today's world, over two thousand years later, perhaps the reason He disappeared at that exact time was to show us that a relationship with

Him is never going to depend on our ability to see Him, but rather upon taking Him at His word.

Now look finally at the response of these two followers of Jesus. Once their eyes were opened and they recognized Him, they could not wait to tell everyone that everything Jesus had said about Himself over the past three years was true. Imagine the excitement they must have felt. **They asked each other, "Were not our hearts burning within us while he talked with us on the road and opened the scriptures to us?"** (Luke 24-32 NIV)

Their encounter with the Shepherd had stirred them on the inside. It had moved everything that was in their very being. Perhaps they were remembering everything that had happened over the previous years and seen it all afresh with the knowledge that it had all been true.

As we read on we see that at that very hour, as dark as it was, as late as it was, and almost certainly, how dangerous the road would be, they left their home and village for Jerusalem. They would have shouted aloud and spoken to everyone they knew and could find that Jesus was risen, that He had walked with them and talked with them, that He had revealed Himself through explaining the scriptures to them, and that He had broken bread with them at their table.

The Shepherd today continues to reveal Himself through scripture, and it is the Good News of the Gospel that comforts us and lets us know that no matter what we may do, He will never give up on us.

Questions:

1) How would it feel if you were blind to the spiritual realities of the Kingdom of God? Would such blindness prevent you hearing the Shepherd's voice clearly?

2) What if things don't turn out like you expect? Would you think of giving up and admitting defeat, rather than seeing

things differently; or could you look and see if maybe God is up to something you simply do not understand?

3) Many people today know who Jesus is. You may have heard about Him, read about Him, use His name, and even claim to know Him. The question is, "how would you recognize Him if He revealed Himself to you today?"

CHAPTER 14
THE SHEPHERD AND PETER

We have talked a bit about Peter in Chapter 7, but this was only a flavour of Peter's life with the Shepherd.

Ever since I fell in love with the Shepherd, I have seen Peter's story as the one I felt most reflected my life up to this point in time.

The following story is about myself, and my mum and dad seeing the best in me, when due to my actions, others were not so impressed. It is a story of forgiveness and restoration, which is why I love Peter's story so much.

When I was a young teenager, I spent more time away from my secondary school in Beckenham, South London, than I did in it. I had deliberately failed the Eleven-Plus exams, so that I could go to school with my pals, but once I got to school, I was bored with everything we did other than sport. I loved football, and still do today, with my beloved Crystal Palace football team playing a big part in my life.

To avoid being bored, and as a lover of trains (I know what you are thinking!) of all descriptions, I would purchase a penny platform ticket at my local train station and then ride the trains to wherever I could get. In those days, if you didn't leave the station, nobody questioned what you were doing. So, I thought!

I went all over the place without getting caught, until one day when I was standing on Clapham Junction Railway Station in south London minding my own business, a ticket collector asked to see my ticket. I sheepishly showed him the platform ticket that I had purchased that morning from my local station, which ended up with me being removed from the station and out on to the street. (I realise today that the outcome could have been a lot worse, so I am very grateful to that ticket collector for not taking matters further.)

Other than the penny that I had spent on the platform ticket, I had no money on me when I left home, so therefore had to walk home. It was only about eight miles to walk, and I had plenty of time to get back home at the same time as my younger brother was returning from school.

Later that evening, I remember thinking, "it was a good job that this didn't happen at some of the other stations I had visited, as I could have been 30, 40 or even 50 miles away from home".

In case you are wondering, there is a reason for this story. The next day, my parents received a letter from the school headmaster asking them if their son was ok. The school were concerned about the various illnesses that I had been suffering, and wanted to talk to them about the letters that they had sent to the school. This was a great surprise to my lovely mum and dad as they hadn't written any letters to the school about anything. You guessed it, they all came from me.

All of this ended up with me being expelled from school at the end of that week.

This is where Peter's story comes in for me. Nobody could see any good coming in to my life or indeed from my life. I was a failure, first to the teachers in my school, and secondly, my mum and dad's initial response seemed to be the same as the teachers.

Thankfully, this wasn't the truth. My mum and dad had other thoughts and ideas about their son. They talked together, and then my mum took me to one side and told me that they didn't believe that I had ruined my life. That day, my mum and dad enrolled me into the next term at Ravensbourne College of Art and Design in Bromley, and once I got there, I discovered the forgiveness that my mum and dad had given me, and a future that had both hope and promise.

As you read on, I hope that you see the connection?

The first place in the Bible we get to know Peter, is in the Book of Matthew.

18 As Jesus was walking beside the Sea of Galilee, he saw two brothers, Simon called Peter and his brother Andrew. They were casting a net into the lake, for they were fishermen. 19 'Come, follow me,' Jesus said, 'and I will send you out to fish for people.' 20 At once they left their nets and followed him. (Matthew 4:18-20 NIV)

However, this is not the first time that Peter had met Jesus. John tells us in his gospel:

35 The next day John was there again with two of his disciples. 36 When he saw Jesus passing by, he said, 'Look, the Lamb of God!'

37 When the two disciples heard him say this, they followed Jesus. 38 Turning around, Jesus saw them following and asked, 'What do you want?'

They said, 'Rabbi' (which means 'Teacher'), 'where are you staying?'

39 'Come,' he replied, 'and you will see.'

So they went and saw where he was staying, and they spent that day with him. It was about four in the afternoon.

40 Andrew, Simon Peter's brother, was one of the two who heard what John had said and who had followed Jesus. 41 The first thing Andrew did was to find his brother Simon and tell him, 'We have found the Messiah' (that is, the Christ). 42 And he brought him to Jesus.

Jesus looked at him and said, 'You are Simon son of John. You will be called Cephas' (which, when translated, is Peter). (John 1:35-42 NIV)

The transformation of this man Simon, a Galilean fisherman, to Peter, a leader of the followers of the Shepherd, who was prepared to challenge and defy the Jewish and Roman authorities, is a story of enduring power that has provided hope and inspiration for myself and the followers of Jesus for the last two thousand years or so.

Matthew's description of the call of Peter and Andrew is brief. Jesus sees them, calls them, and they obey. From this account, we can clearly see that it is Jesus who calls, and it is Peter and Andrew who respond to the call.

It is the content of the call that is important; it is first and foremost a call to follow Jesus, to be in relationship with him. This is the foundation of the life that Peter now lives right up to his death. The call to follow Jesus is so important that Jesus' last words to Peter, as set out in John's gospel, are:

22 Jesus answered, "If I want him to remain alive until I return, what is that to you? You must follow me." (John 21:22 NIV)

The Shepherd is seeking a deep relationship with Peter, and it's based upon the fact that Jesus is the Master and Peter is the disciple. The Shepherd here is prophetically calling Peter into a new way of life and living. From this day on he is to be a fisher of men. The Shepherd wants Peter to clearly understand the nature of this new relationship and the overall goal that they are aiming at.

At the beginning of this relationship, it is necessary for us to see how the Shepherd relates to Peter. Peter is one of the 'inner circle' with James and John. They are some of the first followers, and they find themselves getting extra training from Jesus and over the following three years or so, are given the privilege of seeing the raising of the synagogue ruler's daughter from the dead, witnessing the transfiguration, and keeping watch with Jesus in Gethsemane.

One other point here to mention is that Peter, as well as following the Shepherd also hosted Him in his house. The first gift Peter gets from this hosting is the healing of his mother-in-law, and the second is that the front door of his house becomes a meeting place and a hospital and a place where demons are dispatched. What a wonderful thought!

29 As soon as they left the synagogue, they went with James and John to the home of Simon and Andrew. 30 Simon's mother-in-law was in bed with a fever, and they immediately told Jesus about her. 31 So he went to her, took her hand and helped her up. The fever left her, and she began to wait on them.

32 That evening after sunset the people brought to Jesus all the sick and demon-possessed. 33 The whole town gathered at the door, 34 and Jesus healed many who had various diseases. He also drove out many demons, but he would not let the demons speak because they knew who he was. (Mark 1:29-34 NIV)

Notwithstanding all of this, a key moment in this remarkable relationship between Jesus and Peter is Peter's confession.

Peter's amazing confession, is a significant one. The result of this confession is that Jesus appoints Peter to a key role in the Kingdom of Heaven. Jesus again affirms Peter as the rock because Peter understands who Jesus is; it is the depth and quality of Peter's relationship with Jesus, based on the knowledge revealed to him by the Holy Spirit, that makes him perfect for this role.

Peter's strength of character required a sustained training process throughout his time with the Shepherd. The Shepherd had to continually instruct and reinstruct Peter, with at times reinforcing the teaching with times of strong correction. Because of this, we can see the extent of the change that takes place in Peter as he eventually submits to Jesus' will and no longer seeks his own glory.

As we look further at the relationship between the two of them, we come to the strange story of 'walking on water', and we see Peter's strength of character come to the fore once again.

Remember that the disciples were experienced fishermen who knew the waters they were on like the backs of their hands. Now they are in the middle of a violent storm, and have been struggling with the bad weather for many hours. When Jesus approaches them, it is between 3 a.m. and 6 a.m. They were almost certainly physically exhausted from their fight with the storm. Their first reaction when they see what they believe to be a ghost approaching, is fear. And why not? In Peter this fear is quickly reversed when he sees that it is Jesus. His first thought is to get to where Jesus is. You might think that this is typical of impulsive Peter, and his request to walk with Jesus on such rough and stormy water just doesn't make sense. Jesus doesn't think like that. The Shepherd doesn't condemn Peter; His only desire is to encourage his faith.

This is the kind of faith that the Shepherd is looking for in those that follow Him.

We can't finish this chapter without looking at Peter's denial of the Shepherd and his final restoration.

Luke's account of the prediction of Peter's denial gives us an insight.

For who is greater, the one who is at the table or the one who serves? Is it not the one who is at the table? But I am among you as one who serves. 28 You are those who have stood by me in my trials. 29 And I confer on you a kingdom, just as my Father conferred one on me, 30 so that you may eat and drink at my table in my kingdom and sit on thrones, judging the twelve tribes of Israel.

31 "Simon, Simon, Satan has asked to sift all of you as wheat. 32 But I have prayed for you, Simon, that your faith may not fail. And when you have turned back, strengthen your brothers."

33 But he replied, "Lord, I am ready to go with you to prison and to death."

34 Jesus answered, "I tell you, Peter, before the rooster crows today, you will deny three times that you know me." (Luke 22:27-34 NIV)

Jesus begins his prediction with the words 'Simon, Simon'. The repetition of his name could well demonstrate a sense of grief, of kindness and of love on behalf of the Shepherd; at this crucial time in His ministry here on the earth, Jesus seems to be particularly moved by the trial that he knows Peter will undergo in the coming hours. The Shepherd's use of Simon, rather than Peter, could well underline this. All of Simon's progress towards becoming Peter will be knocked back in this one incident in time and geography.

Jesus has prayed for Simon, especially that his faith will not fail. Jesus is desperate to guard his ongoing relationship with Peter, which, at the time of his testing, and in the future, will be based upon faith alone.

Luke writing in his gospel is crystal clear: Peter will survive the ordeal because Jesus has prayed for him. It displays one of the ways in which his relationship with Peter and his relationship with the Father interact. Jesus is particularly concerned for Peter in his coming trial, as he will be the only disciple to betray Jesus in public like that. Can you imagine what that might mean for Peter?

Jesus must also be concerned that Peter will come through his ordeal and become the rock that the Shepherd said he would be. The Shepherd is trusting that His friend and follower will overcome his act of betrayal. His desire would be that Peter would have been reassured that, although Jesus knew in advance of his betrayal, it did not disqualify him from a relationship with the Shepherd.

Jesus' concern and love for Peter is again shown in his post-resurrection conversation in John 21.

15 When they had finished eating, Jesus said to Simon Peter, "Simon son of John, do you love me more than these?"

"Yes, Lord," he said, "you know that I love you."

Jesus said, "Feed my lambs."

16 Again Jesus said, "Simon son of John, do you love me?"

He answered, "Yes, Lord, you know that I love you."

Jesus said, "Take care of my sheep."

17 The third time he said to him, "Simon son of John, do you love me?"

Peter was hurt because Jesus asked him the third time, "Do you love me?" He said, "Lord, you know all things; you know that I love you."

Jesus said, "Feed my sheep". (John 21:15-17 NIV)

The Shepherd takes the time to reinstate Peter and demonstrate His forgiveness. Although Peter is clearly hurt by Jesus' third repetition of his question 'Do you love me?', Jesus is gently forcing a threefold declaration of his love that mirrors Peter's threefold denial.

The repetition brings about Peter's declaration, 'Lord you know all things…' and we see him throwing himself utterly and completely in reliance on Jesus.

Can you see and feel the progress in Peter's relationship with Jesus? In full restoration, Peter now responds in a more appropriate way than he did on so many previous occasions on his journey.

It is an awesome thought that throughout time, God has placed the future of mankind in the hands of ordinary men and women like Peter, and it is good to know that right now, our heavenly priest, Jesus, sits at the right hand of The Father interceding for all of us.

It really doesn't matter what you have done or not done in your life. No-one is beyond the redemptive love of the Saviour.

The Shepherd, through the writings of His servant Peter, continues to speak today into the lives of those who would listen, and if they obey the instructions, their lives will be forever changed.

There are benefits from hearing and responding to the voice of the Shepherd and there are consequences from not doing so.

Questions:

1) **What are the two most interesting lessons that you have learnt through the story of the Shepherd and Peter?**

2) **How would you feel if you found yourself in a situation where you thought that you couldn't stand up for the Shepherd, or that you even deny Him? Can you in your mind's eye, remember that He sits at the right hand of His Father interceding for you, declaring that you are His brother or sister, and that He is not ashamed of you?**

CHAPTER 15
THE SHEPHERD AND PAUL

God the Father, God the Son and God the Holy Spirit, since the beginning of time, seem to have had to put up with mankind's disobedience and complete rejection of their heartfelt intention to have everlasting relationship with those they had created.

Story after story, throughout the entire Old Testament period, talks of mankind seeking their own way, following and worshipping their own gods and generally being hostile to the desires of the God of creation.

In the New Testament, the Son of God, Jesus, was born with a price on His head, and with His family, had to flee Israel and spend the first years of his earthly life in a foreign land. If you like, as an illegal immigrant in that land.

So, rejection and utter contempt was not unusual for the Shepherd to experience. Just look at the build up to the cross!

So, it comes to the man known as Saul of Tarsus, who had the job of persecuting the followers of Jesus, known at the time as 'Followers of the Way'.

The first we hear about Saul is when we read about Stephen in the Book of Acts. Stephen is stoned to death because of his witness to the Messiah, and it says, **they rushed at him, dragged him out of the city and began** to stone him. Meanwhile, the witnesses laid their coats at the feet of a young man named Saul. (Acts 7:58 N I V)

It goes on to say, ...Saul approved of their killing him. On that day a great persecution broke out against the church in Jerusalem, and all except the apostles were scattered throughout Judea and Samaria. Godly men buried Stephen and mourned deeply for him. But Saul began to destroy the church. Going from house to house, he dragged off both men and women and put them in prison. (Acts 8:1-3 N I V)

Just a note here – if you think that your behaviour precludes you from hearing the voice of the Shepherd, please read on.

Saul is on his way, with letters from the high Priest, to the synagogues in Damascus, to arrest any that he found there who were followers of 'The Way'. As he nears Damascus, the following happens:

3 As he neared Damascus on his journey, suddenly a light from heaven flashed around him. 4 He fell to the ground and heard a voice say to him, "Saul, Saul, why do you persecute me?"

5 "Who are you, Lord?" Saul asked.

"I am Jesus, whom you are persecuting," he replied. 6 "Now get up and go into the city, and you will be told what you must do."

7 The men traveling with Saul stood there speechless; they heard the sound but did not see anyone. 8 Saul got up from the ground, but when he opened his eyes he could see nothing. So they led him by the hand into Damascus. 9 For three days he was blind, and did not eat or drink anything. (Acts 9:3-9 NIV)

Saul's job was to persecute the church, and we need to remember that the followers of the Shepherd in those early days did not have the New Testament in written word, they were following presumably, through testimony and experience. Saul could not have believed that Israel's

Messiah had come, which was why he was trying to shut down the gatherings of this misguided people.

Saul could not have believed for a minute that he was persecuting the God of Israel, whom he loved with a passion, so therefore this confrontation with the Shepherd must have been the most confusing minute of his life. He believed that he was persecuting a misguided people, not persecuting God.

It is easy for us with hindsight to see what was going on, but how could Saul equate what he was doing with the High Priest's approval with persecuting God?

Jesus is clear in His statement. "You persecute my church – you persecute Me".

What is Saul to make of his blind state for three days, and his first hearing of the Shepherd's voice? I guess if it was you or me, we would probably fall on our faces in fear. The Bible is silent on Saul's thoughts, so we can only imagine what he was thinking.

This won't be the last time that the Shepherd speaks to Saul, but to add some spice to the mix, He decides to use a follower of 'The Way' to bring the next conversation into Saul's life.

10 In Damascus there was a disciple named Ananias. The Lord called to him in a vision, "Ananias!"

"Yes, Lord," he answered.

11 The Lord told him, "Go to the house of Judas on Straight Street and ask for a man from Tarsus named Saul, for he is praying. 12 In a vision he has seen a man named Ananias come and place his hands on him to restore his sight."

13 "Lord," Ananias answered, "I have heard many reports about this man and all the harm he has done to your holy people in Jerusalem.

14 And he has come here with authority from the chief priests to arrest all who call on your name."

15 But the Lord said to Ananias, "Go! This man is my chosen instrument to proclaim my name to the Gentiles and their kings and to the people of Israel. 16 I will show him how much he must suffer for my name."

17 Then Ananias went to the house and entered it. Placing his hands on Saul, he said, "Brother Saul, the Lord—Jesus, who appeared to you on the road as you were coming here—has sent me so that you may see again and be filled with the Holy Spirit." 18 Immediately, something like scales fell from Saul's eyes, and he could see again. He got up and was baptized, 19 and after taking some food, he regained his strength. Saul spent several days with the disciples in Damascus. (Acts 9:10-19 NIV)

One of the very people that Saul had been sent to arrest, now brings the Shepherd's instructions which will release Saul, later to be called Paul, to fulfil the call that the Shepherd has placed on his life.

Paul's life story is too much for this book, but a few examples will show us how the Shepherd guided him on his way.

In Acts chapters 13 and 14, we read about Paul's first missionary journey. It is in the church at Antioch where we hear about God's directions for both him and Barnabas.

1 Now in the church at Antioch there were prophets and teachers: Barnabas, Simeon called Niger, Lucius of Cyrene, Manaen (who had been brought up with Herod the tetrarch) and Saul. 2 While they were worshipping the Lord and fasting, the Holy Spirit said, 'Set apart for me Barnabas and Saul for the work to which I have called them.' 3 So after they had fasted and prayed, they placed their hands on them and sent them off. (Acts 13:1-3 NIV)

The NIV Study Bible notes on verse 2 are very helpful here – 'Paul's first missionary journey did not result from a planning session but from the Spirit's initiative as the leaders worshipped. The communication from the Holy Spirit *may* have come through the prophets. (Italics are mine)

The Shepherd has a job for Paul to do, which will last until He returns in His glory and majesty. It starts here in Antioch, which is an ancient Syrian town, now known as Antakya, a major town of south-central Turkey.

Off to Cyprus where Saul takes on the name of Paul, then onto Perga in Pamphylia, on the southern coast of modern day Turkey. Next, the two go to Pisidian Antioch, about 110 miles. Today the ruins of Pisidian Antioch lie about a mile north of the modern town of Yalvaç. This is where we hear Paul's first recorded sermon. Here the Jewish people get a history lesson about their God.

10 'Fellow Israelites and you Gentiles who worship God, listen to me! 17 The God of the people of Israel chose our ancestors; he made the people prosper during their stay in Egypt; with mighty power he led them out of that country; 18 for about forty years he endured their conduct in the wilderness; 19 and he overthrew seven nations in Canaan, giving their land to his people as their inheritance. 20 All this took about 450 years.

'After this, God gave them judges until the time of Samuel the prophet. 21 Then the people asked for a king, and he gave them Saul son of Kish, of the tribe of Benjamin, who ruled for forty years. 22 After removing Saul, he made David their king. God testified concerning him: "I have found David son of Jesse, a man after my own heart; he will do everything I want him to do."

23 'From this man's descendants God has brought to Israel the Saviour Jesus, as he promised. 24 Before the coming of Jesus, John preached repentance and baptism to all the people of Israel. 25 As John was completing his work, he said: "Who do you suppose I am?

Ron Warren

I am not the one you are looking for. But there is one coming after me whose sandals I am not worthy to untie."

26 'Fellow children of Abraham and you God-fearing Gentiles, it is to us that this message of salvation has been sent. 27 The people of Jerusalem and their rulers did not recognise Jesus, yet in condemning him they fulfilled the words of the prophets that are read every Sabbath. 28 Though they found no proper ground for a death sentence, they asked Pilate to have him executed. 29 When they had carried out all that was written about him, they took him down from the cross and laid him in a tomb. 30 But God raised him from the dead, 31 and for many days he was seen by those who had travelled with him from Galilee to Jerusalem. They are now his witnesses to our people.

32 'We tell you the good news: what God promised our ancestors 33 he has fulfilled for us, their children, by raising up Jesus. As it is written in the second Psalm:

'"You are my son; today I have become your father."

34 God raised him from the dead so that he will never be subject to decay. As God has said,

'"I will give you the holy and sure blessings promised to David."
(Acts 13:16-34 NIV)

Can you see what is happening here? Paul, having had a complete 180 degrees turn in his understanding of God, is having the same effect on the Jewish leaders as Stephen did when he addressed the Sanhedrin, as recorded in the Book of Acts, chapter seven. The very statements that led to Stephen's stoning, are now fully understood and accepted by Paul as the truth.

Paul's life after this is a model of what it looks like to listen to the voice of the Shepherd and do what He says to do.

For an example of this life of following the Shepherd, just look at a small but not insignificant incident reported in the Book of Acts chapter 16.

6 Paul and his companions travelled throughout the region of Phrygia and Galatia, having been kept by the Holy Spirit from preaching the word in the province of Asia. 7 When they came to the border of Mysia, they tried to enter Bithynia, but the Spirit of Jesus would not allow them to. 8 So they passed by Mysia and went down to Troas. 9 During the night Paul had a vision of a man of Macedonia standing and begging him, "Come over to Macedonia and help us." 10 After Paul had seen the vision, we got ready at once to leave for Macedonia, concluding that God had called us to preach the gospel to them. (Acts 16:6-10 NIV)

First the call, but just as important, the response. *"We got ready at once to leave for Macedonia."*

I mentioned before about a ministry trip that I led, which was to the north-west area of Bulgaria with my friend John and others. This came about after I heard an interview with a Bulgarian pastor on BBC radio, whilst driving my car. He was being asked about the conditions in Bulgarian orphanages. The pastor's response was, "The world thinks that Romanian orphanages are the only ones that need help. They certainly need that help, but they're not the only ones. Because of our Government, most people do not know about the state of ours here in Bulgaria. We need the same level of assistance and support, and if anyone is listening, could you please come and help?"

When I heard this, I thought, "I am listening, I will go." Later that day, I had a conversation with my then church leader, Andrew Proctor, who's immediate response was to hand me 1,000 US Dollars from church funds, with an instruction to take a team and do what we could do to help.

To this day, we still have friends in that Bulgarian town of Vidin.

For the rest of his earthly life, Paul went wherever he was sent, and he fought for the gospel wherever it was rejected, or where legalism raised its ugly head from the religious leaders, to put obstacles in the way. (I know that every uncircumcised male follower of the Shepherd today is grateful that Paul won the argument about circumcision!)

It is encouraging to all of us, that over the last two thousand years or so, followers of the Shepherd have been doing the same thing as Paul did, furthering the gospel in every corner of the world, overcoming opposition wherever they come up against it.

The Shepherd, through the writings of His servant Paul, continues to speak today into the lives of those who would listen, and if they obey the instructions, their lives will be forever changed.

There are benefits from hearing and responding to the voice of the Shepherd and there are consequences from not doing so.

Questions:

1) How would it feel to hear the Shepherd as clearly as Paul did? If this is something you desire, then I suggest that, just like Samuel, you ask Him to "Speak Lord, for your servant is listening."

2) What would it look like today responding to the Shepherd in the way Paul did? If it helps, just listen again to Mary's words to the servants, "Whatever He tells you to do, do it."

Chapter 16

THE SHEPHERD AND JOHN

We can look all over the gospels to find the relationship between the Shepherd and John, however it seems only right and proper to look first at John's own gospel and his letters to begin to discover what was going on.

The NIV Study Bible helpfully states in its notes about the author of the 'Gospel of John', and the 'Letters of John', that the author is the apostle John, "the disciple whom Jesus loved" (John 13:23, 19:26' 20:2, 21:7,20,24). At the beginning of the letter '1 John', the note goes on to say that this John is the son of Zebedee (Mark 1:19-20), he was a first cousin of Jesus (his mother was Salome, a sister of Mary (Mark 16:1, John 19:25), he was a fisherman and one of Jesus' inner circle together with James and Peter.

Some theologians would say that this John was probably not the writer of the Book of Revelation, known as 'John the Seer' or 'John the Divine'. So, to understand the relationship between the Shepherd and John, we can only legitimately look at what I have said above.

There seems to be a special relationship between the Shepherd and John, which is revealed only in John's gospel, when John talks about 'the disciple whom Jesus loved'. We find all the references to "the disciple whom Jesus loved" in John 13:23, John 19:26, John 20:2, John 21:7, and John 21:20.

The first question we should ask is, why does John term himself as the "disciple whom Jesus loved?" Maybe it was his way of showing what is true of all disciples. We are all to find our identity first and foremost in the fact that Jesus loves us. If you were to ask John who he is, he probably would not answer by giving his name, John, his family connections, that he is related to Jesus, or his occupation, a fisherman. He would respond, I am sure, by saying, "I am someone Jesus loves."

In one of his sermons, C. H. Spurgeon said this about John, **the disciple whom Jesus loved, is a name which John gives to himself. I think he repeats it five times. No other writer calls John, "the disciple whom Jesus loved." John has thus surnamed himself and all the early writers recognize him under that title. Do not suspect him, however, of egotism. It is one of the instances in which egotism is quite out of the question. Naturally, you and I would be rather slow to take such a title, even if we felt it belonged to us because we would be jealous for our reputation and be afraid of being thought presumptuous. But with a sweet naiveté which makes him quite forget himself, John took the name which he knew most accurately described him, whether others quibbled at it or not.**

So far from there being any pride in it, it just shows the simplicity of his spirit, the openness, the transparency of his character and his complete self-forgetfulness. Knowing it to be the truth, he does not hesitate to say it. He was sure that Jesus loved him better than others and, though he marvelled at it more than anyone else, yet he so rejoiced in the fact that he could not help publishing it, whatever the consequences might be. Often there is a deal more pride in not witnessing to what God has done for us than in speaking of it. Everything depends upon the spirit which moves us.

When I was a young teenager living in South London, I would play football with my mates, and if it was light enough to see the goals, the game would go on into the late evening. My mates and football were the only thing that mattered to me. They were good mates. It is a great game.

When I was thirteen, my mum and dad joined a 'self-build' group, building eighteen houses in the village of West Kingsdown, in Kent, and every weekend I would travel with my dad to do whatever a young boy could do to help with the work. This is where you could say, that I was a bit slow on the uptake? One Friday night, after getting back from playing football with my mates, I saw my uncle's fish lorry outside our flat, with what looked like our furniture tied on the back. On asking what was going on, my mum and dad informed me that our new house was finished, and we were moving to it first thing in the morning!

The point of this story is that I did not get a chance to say goodbye to my great mates, and the reality is, I haven't seen them or spoken to them to this day.

That left quite an emotional scar.

I have mentioned my very dear friend, Terry, before, and this is where the story continues.

Other than work mates, or friends of my wife Jo, since the day leaving South London, I hadn't had a very close friend who I could just hang out with. Out of the blue, after meeting Liz, Terry's wife, I met Terry. This man became the best friend that I have ever had. Whether we were talking about faith matters, the difference between Chelsea Football Club and Crystal Palace football club, sharing holidays together with our respective families or just hanging out, I had at last found what I had lost the day we left our home in South London and headed for Kent. I would describe myself as Terry's friend, and describe Terry as my best friend.

You can imagine, I am sure, how I felt the day Terry went to be with the Shepherd?

In the depths of my anger and sadness, I sensed the Shepherd say, I want you to study and look at My servant, John. After reading everything that John had written in the Bible, I again sensed the Shepherd say, I am like that for you. I am closer to you than any earthly friend could ever be. Stay close to me and you will never be alone again, ever. You are my beloved. I love you. Wow.

That has been my experience with the Shepherd ever since. I describe myself as John might do, "I am someone Jesus loves."

What is the Shepherd saying to His followers today, through His servant John?

I once heard a preacher say to every individual in the hall, "you are His favourite." At the time, this didn't make too much sense to me, but now I do understand. As with John, the preacher was saying it was his way of showing what is true of all disciples. We are His favourite. I have since seen the movie of 'The Shack', in which God says that He is especially fond of the person He was talking to. An amazing understanding of the love of our heavenly Father.

We are all to find our identity first and foremost in the fact that Jesus loves us. He loves us so much that He came out of glory for each one, and died the most awful death in our place, to bring us back into a right relationship with our heavenly Father. What a friend.

Perhaps you need to hear this today – 'Jesus loves you'.

This love that Jesus has for each of us is unconditional. It exists even if we do not acknowledge Him. It exists even if we have rejected Him. Please hear this – Jesus' love for us exists today, no matter what.

Like John, do you know that you can delight the King of heaven today?

I love the following quote from Chaim Bentorah in his book, titled 'A Hebrew Teacher Explores the Heart of God' (20):

For love to be completed, it must be returned. Love can be lonely and painful if it is not returned. A young teenage girl can moon over some handsome dude who doesn't even know she is alive and feel depressed, sad and broken hearted. But if that skinny little teenage guy looks

into her eyes and says: "I love you," she is immediately transported to cloud nine, where birds sing, and flowers look beautiful again.

Love can exist if it is not returned, but it cannot sing until it is shared.

God loves the world, but the world does not love Him in return. It is when we love Him in return that His love is complete. It is when we love Him in return that He can rejoice over us with singing. (Zephaniah 3:17)

Salvation is not just about getting saved and going to be with Him, it is about completing the love that God has for us, bringing that joy and celebration to the heart of God that has been mooning over us since the beginning of time, just like that teenage girl.

Why do you think the angels rejoice over one sinner that repents? It is the same reason that you might cry at a wedding. You are rejoicing over seeing two people who have found each other in love and share that love and return that love to each other.

Just like a good rom-com, the angels rejoice because they love a good romance story where two people love each other.

It is not that God loves one person more than the other, He loves all equally. It is just that very few will love Him in return and complete His love, bringing Him the joy of His love, and cause Him to sing with joy in that love.

It is amazing that you and I, simple frail little human beings, can bring joy to the God of the Universe by simply saying: "I love You." Have you told Him today that you love Him?

Do you want to give the all mighty, all powerful God a thrill and make His day?

Tell Him you love Him.

There is not just a passion in God's heart to love, although it is there, there is also a longing in His heart to be loved in return.

The Shepherd says to all that follow Him and love Him completely, "It is your absolute right to see yourself as the disciple whom Jesus loves, and to call yourself that!"

The Shepherd, through the writings of His servant John, continues to speak today into the lives of those who would listen, and if they hear what He says, their lives will be forever changed, and they will never be alone again.

There are benefits from hearing and responding to the voice of the Shepherd and there are consequences from not doing so.

Questions:

1) How would you feel if you knew deep within your heart, the Shepherd loves you as much as He did His servant, John?

2) Do you want to respond to the Shepherd as John did? If so, ask Him to reveal Himself to you like He did to His servant John.

CHAPTER 17
THE SHEPHERD AND HIS CHURCH

Before I set out what I think the Shepherd is saying, the one thing I know for certain is that Jesus doesn't see the church as we maybe see it. For Jesus, His church worldwide and throughout history is one entity, drawn together under His kingship. It is not a host of different churches. Yes, His church is made up of different parts, which meets in different places throughout the world, and these separate parts must be led by local shepherds who have been called to fulfil Jesus' feet washing instructions.

Now the time has come to expand on this chapter, and I confess it is with some trepidation, but I always remember the phrase that I heard John Wimber say, the first time I heard him speak at the Wembley Conference Centre.

John said, "he loved the church in all of its forms, and he said he prayed for them and honoured every church on the earth that declared publicly that 'Jesus is Lord'". John also said that "if we could see what Jesus was doing in His church, we would be surprised, and maybe not even believe all that we heard".

I absolutely agree with all that John said. Whilst leading the Vineyard in Dartford, Jo and I would insist that the church would pray for every church in the town on a regular basis, and that we would take an active role in seeking to bless and work with the other churches under the heading of 'Churches Together in Dartford'.

It didn't matter to us what their non-essential beliefs were, or even how they worked out their churchmanship with the followers of Jesus who were with them in this place in time and geography. If they honoured Jesus as the Son of God, The King of Heaven and the Saviour of the world, we were with them.

As Augustine of Hippo so wonderfully said, *"In essentials, unity; in non-essentials, liberty; in all things, charity."*

We might think all sorts of things about the church today. It may seem to us at best to be like a dysfunctional family, it may even look at times like some parts of the church are at war with other parts of the church, and you could be anywhere on that crazy spectrum at any given time in your life. The truth is, that no matter what we might think, Jesus loves His bride, the church, and He is coming back for her, and I believe that the Shepherd is telling us to reflect deeply on the words of Augustine of Hippo above.

My friend, Jamie Stilson says the following in his book, 'The Power of Ugly' (8), **It's so easy to judge the church with all her weaknesses. Some people write books about them, making a living by bashing the church, but it is still the Bride of Christ, which He laid His life down to save; and in His eyes, she is beautiful! So, before you start judging the church (which takes very little intelligence to do, since the flaws are many, and obvious), remember that this is your family too. So, grow up, learn some humility, get the "... plank out of your own eye, and then you will see clearly to remove the speck from your brother's eye" (Matthew 7:5). Jamie finishes this little word with the following, "The greatest thing that is wrong with the church is me and you!**

This last part reflects what the writer G. K. Chesterton sent to the London Times newspaper, when they asked some writers of the day for essays on the topic, 'What's wrong with the World?'

His response was the shortest and most to the point:

Dear Sirs,

I am.

Sincerely Yours, G. K. Chesterton.

How true. Not just G. K. Chesterton but me and you too.

As John Mumford would repeatedly say to all the pastors of the Vineyard churches in the UK and Ireland, 'The Vineyard is just another flavour in the wonderful taste that is the church that Jesus loves, and is preparing for eternity'.

We don't have to look far to see what the Shepherd has to say to the church. In the second and third chapters of the Book of Revelation, we can see exactly what He has to say.

According to the NIV Study Bible, the general pattern in the letters written to the seven historic churches in Asia Minor is, '**commendation, complaint and correction**'. (NIV Study Bible notes)

There are many excellent study and lifestyle books that have been written on this vast subject, and probably some of the best sermons ever delivered throughout time, and therefore I can't add any original thoughts on the subject. However, it is good to remind ourselves that the Shepherd commends the churches for their hard work and perseverance, their steadfastness to faith and His name, and their love, faith and service for His cause.

The question remains, is the Shepherd still speaking to both the local and worldwide church today? I believe the answer to this question is yes.

To help me explain what I think the Shepherd is saying today, I am indebted to a Q & A session in the Vineyard Churches USA 'Cutting Edge' magazine titled 'The Church of Jesus is the Hope of the World'

(6) with Bert Waggoner on the subject of 'THE CHURCH LOCAL / THE CHURCH UNIVERSAL'.

(Bert Waggoner was the National Director of the Association of Vineyard Churches USA from 2000 to January 2013.)

Bert Waggoner said the following with regards to the local church, 'In the New Testament, the primary focus is on the local church. That means the full expression of the church, in a real sense, is in the local church. The part is equal to the whole when the New Testament speaks about it. Each local church possesses not a fragment of Christ but the whole of Christ'.

This statement helps me to understand that the Shepherd is saying to every local expression of church, you have all of me. Do not worry, there is nothing missing.

Bert Waggoner goes on to say, 'Historically, the creeds give definition to what constitutes the church, and I think it's hard to improve on what they say. The Apostle's Creed describes the church as: "One, holy, catholic, apostolic." I think all of those are essential marks of a true church. These are the things that must be evident in a group of people to properly be called a church of Jesus Christ.'

This statement underscores what I believe the Shepherd is saying to the worldwide church. "Come together in Me in unity, not uniformity, and do the things that I have asked you to do for the sake of the people of all the Nations, and for the glory of my Father in Heaven."

Eugene Peterson, in his book entitled 'Reversed Thunder' (7), says this, The Gospel is never for individuals but always for people. Sin fragments. It separates us and sends us to some solitary confinement. Gospel restores us, unites us, and sets us in community. The life of faith reveals the nurtured in the biblical narratives as highly personal but never merely individual. Always there is family, a tribe, a nation, a church.

He goes on to say, **the gospel pulls us into community. One of the immediate changes that the gospel makes is grammatical. We instead of I, our instead of my, us instead of me.**

In the fragmented way people live, work and play today, this is what the Shepherd says to all mankind......

WE........OUR........US

Please do not listen to the enemy lie that unity is all about being the same as each other, as if we were clones of some master plan. No. It's about the Shepherd and His calling to absolutely everyone that He has uniquely made in His own image, to go to the ends of the earth proclaiming freedom and bringing hope to a broken world.

On the thought of the Shepherd talking seriously to His church, I am reminded of the prophetic word that Barry Kissell gave at the New Wine Christian Conference in the U.K. about twenty-five years ago. Barry pleaded with every church leader in the tent, to somehow find enough money in their budgets to employ a youth pastor/worker. He said that this was a direct instruction from the throne of God. He then said, the coming battle would be for the youth of our nation.

It doesn't take much imagination to see that this is what has been happening, both in the United Kingdom and around the world.

I am convinced that the leaders in the tent that night, responded to that word, and the outcome is that the church in the United Kingdom today, has many wonderful youth pastors and workers, doing amazing work amongst young people in our villages, towns and cities. However, there is still more to do.

As part of the Dartford Churches Together leadership team, I asked the church leaders in the town to consider providing an independent space, where all the young followers of the Shepherd in the town, no matter which church they belonged to, could meet, and recognise each other. The point I sensed the Shepherd was highlighting, was that in the school classroom, a young follower of His, because of peer pressure, may not know that there are others in the same room who follow Him.

With drug abuse, self-harming, inappropriate sexual activity, peer pressure, social media abuse and all manner of other things that the enemy is throwing at them, the young people of our nation need help. It would be extremely helpful if young people who follow the Shepherd, could confide in their friends at school who might not be so public in their faith, about the challenges they face today. Because the church that their friends and fellow students are part of is different from their own, they may never know that they too are followers of the Shepherd.

Imagine what the classroom would feel like, if it was known that there was more than just one follower of the Shepherd in the room? They will be there, because I believe what the Shepherd says, but the young people might not know that this is the truth.

This suggested initiative was not about 'Youth Work' as we might know it, it was about revealing the truth about what the Shepherd is doing amongst the young people of the town.

The response to this initiative seemed to me to be lukewarm, at best. I think the problem was that they thought it would cut across the wonderful youth work that the different churches were already doing in the town, and it looked like they were concerned that if we did this, it would result in them losing their young people to other, so called, 'happening churches', or worse still in their thought process, losing them to a new 'Youth Church', in the town.

The Shepherd's initiative had nothing to do with the churches in the town. He was pointing to the young people in the area, and the challenges that they face today.

So often fear gets in the way if we think that what we are doing is being replaced by something new from another provider. Having now left the area, I seem to be forever praying for the young people of that town. May God bless them richly.

Another area to look at, is churches are supposed to be 'All Age', 'All Skin Colour', 'All Ability', 'All Social Backgrounds'. The Bride of Christ is called to be inclusive, not exclusive. It has always been its calling to welcome the stranger, the outcast, the rich, the poor, the troubled, the one that doesn't fit, the free, the prisoner, the widow and the orphan.

It is the world that tells us otherwise. It is the world that says, 'this is not supposed to happen'. The calling from the Shepherd is the complete opposite to what the world is saying. Following this call is certainly hard work. It can be difficult, and yes, we are talking about people, with all their varying approaches to life. But the call is the call.

Can you hear the Shepherd calling? **'You who are older, make room for the young, and you who are younger, listen to those who are older than you. You who are included, make room for those who are on the edge of society, and you who are rich, make way for the poor.'**

If you are concerned about losing your position or influence, I believe the Shepherd would say to you, "I tell you, no one is standing behind you, waiting to do the work that I have given you to do, and there is no one standing in the wings waiting for you to fail. If there is somebody like that around you, then rest assured that they have not been sent by me, and I will reveal their plans to you, all in good time".

Finally, it is good for us to remember the Shepherd's prayer to His Father, about the unity of the body, which to date, I believe, has not been fulfilled in the way the Shepherd means it to be.

'I will remain in the world no longer, but they are still in the world, and I am coming to you. Holy Father, protect them by the power of your name, the name you gave me, so that they may be one as we are one.'
(John 17:11 NIV)

There are benefits from hearing and responding to the voice of the Shepherd and there are consequences from not doing so.

Ron Warren

Questions:

1) Are you in leadership in the local church? If the answer is yes, are you honouring the other fellowships who proclaim Jesus as the saviour of the world? What would you say, and how could you improve on what you currently do?

2) Do you believe in community and doing life with others in the church you call home? Do you think - *We* instead of *I*, *our* instead of *my*, *us* instead of *me*?

CHAPTER 18
THE SHEPHERD AND DISCIPLESHIP

This is a huge subject, and to my mind, often misunderstood by many. (Who are you, you might say, to make such statements? I would probably agree with you, but nonetheless I am going to unpack what I think the Shepherd is saying.)

What was Jesus instructing His followers to do, and how did He go about it?

I believe that Jesus made it clear to His disciples, that they were to 'make disciples'. That was their job, and by extension, I passionately believe that it is the same life-giving instruction He gives to His followers today.

The method Jesus showed the early disciples to follow was His own lifestyle. The Shepherd took them to one side, a place of safety if you like, and taught them all about Himself. They were captivated by His story, left everything they had and then followed Him.

The great commission Jesus had imparted to His followers, was not, however, for themselves, although they clearly benefitted from being with Him and following His instructions. Fundamentally, what Jesus was giving them, was an outward looking commission. I am sure that you must have heard the modern version of this – *'The church is the only club for non-members'*?

I have a growing feeling that as we make disciples of Jesus, we become more of the person Jesus designed us to be. You can see from the Book of Acts in the Bible, that as His followers went about sharing their faith in the Messiah. thousands of early seekers were transformed into His disciples, and lives were changed for ever.

As new church pastors, Jo and I attended a conference designed to encourage us in the management of church life, which included everything from United Kingdom Charity Law through to 'Welcome Teams' in church on Sunday mornings. It was a very good conference, and the things that we learnt have stood us in good stead down the years.

Towards the end of the second day, we had an opportunity to ask questions of each other, so that we could receive mutual encouragement. I had a question that had been with me since the beginning of the church plant in Dartford, which I asked. The question was, **'What do you do in your church fellowships, regarding discipleship?'**

There was silence for a minute or so, and then one by one the other church leaders started talking about the courses they were running on the subject. There were as many courses as there were church leaders. Being new, I asked them what the basis of the various courses were, and it seemed to me that they majored on The Father, Son and Holy Spirit, the spiritual disciplines, church membership and inevitably, financial giving.

Of course, none of this is wrong, and I mention here again, the wonderful 'ALPHA' course, which in my opinion, is a crucial tool for those seeking the meaning of life and for young followers of the Shepherd seeking to know more about Him. The problem for me with discipleship courses, was that it didn't seem to produce what Jesus had asked His followers to do, that is, make disciples who follow Him. Listening to the other church leaders, it was clear that the courses were popular, and that people were learning all about discipleship, but when I asked them if those who had been on the course were themselves discipling others, it seemed that what was expected of those who had been on the course, was to invite their friends on to the next one.

I suspect that one of the reasons, we as church leaders, use the discipleship course route, is because we know that people most often have very messy lives. (Of course, that couldn't possibly be us, could it?)

Lots of people encountering Jesus' church today, do not understand who Jesus is, other than perhaps as a baby in a manger or a figure on a cross, nor do they understand what He is doing in the world in which they live, work and play.

Usually, the first people followers of the Shepherd meet, will either be in their family, or their friend who invites them to church, or if they have walked into church on a Sunday morning out of curiosity, the welcome team at the door. Can you see the importance of being a disciple?

Once someone turns to Jesus and starts following Him, and I think of myself here, they do not often bear any resemblance to Him. Because of their very recent past, they can have their head turned by powerful personalities, they might use dodgy business methods, they could be in – or from – broken families, they might be sexually active outside of marriage, maybe they haven't got a clue about sung worship, (I remember someone once ask me why we had karaoke at the start of our service!) or they may have deeply imbedded responses to the culture from where they came.

We will get into their understanding of core doctrine and values towards the end of the chapter.

I can hear some asking, this wouldn't happen in a church, would it?

Forget the church today, just look at the early church in Corinth. That church had all the above. It wasn't a fake church, or a badly run church. It was an authentic gathering of people that the King of Heaven loved. Warts and all.

171

That should open our eyes to what a disciple's job is. A follower of the Shepherd discipling another follower of the Shepherd.

I don't know who described discipleship as "becoming a complete and competent follower of Jesus Christ?" but in writing this book, I certainly wish I had!

Someone else said that a disciple is at heart, a learner who has a servant heart and is called to a life of discipleship, that imitates the life of the Shepherd.

I believe that the core of what Jesus was instructing His followers to do, was to intentionally train people who were voluntarily submitting their lives to His lordship, so that they in turn will train others.

Certainly, Jesus' first disciples seemed desperate to want to imitate Him in every thought, word, and deed, and when they seemed to succeed in it, amazing things happened around them. I can't help but believe that they sought to train others who followed, in the same way.

What was it that they saw? They saw that Jesus' teaching was most effective when He gathered His followers for meals, when He welcomed sinners and when He healed those who were brought to him. He challenged the status quo, took time off by himself for prayer, went away from the crowds with his disciples so that He could explain to them in more detail about His ministry, and what I think must have been the scariest thing of all, His followers saw the amazing miracles of provision, healing and creation obedience.

All the foregoing is fundamental for the church's work in helping the King of Heaven to expand the Kingdom of God here in our world.

If, like me, you love the world in which you live, how can you ignore all that the Shepherd has instructed us to do?

Regarding core values and doctrines, we need to show others, as disciples ourselves, who Jesus is. If you study the life of Jesus, you will see the whole reason behind why He came was love. Jesus said that love will be the authentic mark of those who follow Him. Jesus explained that the relationship between God the Father, God the Son and God the Holy Spirit, is love. Jesus showed to His followers that the relationship between the Godhead and humanity is based on the same foundation, love. The Kingdom He ushered in is a Kingdom of love.

From this you will see that the motivation for both evangelism and discipleship, is the same. Again, as the Beatles sang, Love, Love, Love.

The next question must be, if we follow the Shepherd's instructions, what would it look like today?

First, inside the church.

I can only look at this from my own experience, plus drawing on the experiences of other church leaders that I have a relationship with.

As a church leader, other than the prime calling on my life which is to love God, and make disciples of my friends and family, I have a specific call which is to be a pastor, to shepherd the sheep He has left in my care, and to train leaders who will train leaders.

Training leaders who will train leaders is a wonderful job. First, it is imparting the vision that the Shepherd is revealing to us. Unpacking the thumb print that God has placed on the fellowship. These are critical to the life of the local fellowship. They are basic headings, and individually, they look like this:

Worship Leader – Sung worship must be to Jesus, not about Jesus. It can be both up-tempo and down-tempo, and it can be joyful as well as intimate.

Small Group Overseer – Small groups must be about doing 'life' together, and they must be open and not closed, containing within them some measure of sung worship, shared teaching, prayer and ministry to one another.

Welcome Team Leader – Ensure that everybody who comes into the building is welcomed, and looked after. If the person is new, to hand them on to someone who can help them find refreshments and a seat. If children are with the person, to make sure that they know where and when to go to the creche, Kids church or youth church.

Hospitality team Leader – Ensure that the budget is not exceeded, and that coffee, tea and soft drinks are of the highest quality, and that any snacks are well presented, with the relevant dietary information clearly shown.

Kids Church and Youth church leaders – Ensure that the gospel is presented in an age relevant way, and that the young people are taught how to read the bible, pray and minister to one another, and grow in maturity for their age.

If all the leaders we have are disciples of the Shepherd, they love the Lord their God, they read the bible, pray regularly and give generously to the church, in my understanding, looking at the way Jesus first sent out the twelve and then the seventy-two, our job is to let them get on with what Jesus has asked them to do.

I have never asked a worship leader for a list of songs before a service, never asked to see the details of how small groups are structured, never stood on the shoulders of the welcome team, only ever enjoyed the snacks and drinks that the hospitality team have provided, and cheered on the young people in all that they were doing.

As far as I understand, once leaders know the basis upon which they are leading, my job was to set them free to seek the Holy Spirit in prayer and then carry out whatever He asks them to do. If I pray to the Holy Spirit for direction, then why should I not trust Him to guide others seeking His direction. When Jesus sent the disciples out, it is clear from the Bible that He didn't go with them in person. It is a wonderful model.

I don't doubt that some church leaders will take issue with this, but I can't understand why they would. If we micro manage disciples in the church, how are they ever going to be able to make disciples in the world, without forever seeking approval from their church leaders?

Second, outside the church and into the world.

I am reminded of a Dartford church leader telling me about how a visiting preacher at the beginning of his sermon, threw an orange at the pristine white wall of the church building. I am not sure if the church members were that happy at what had gone on, but the church leader was overjoyed. The point the visiting preacher was making was that the lovely white walls were stopping the gospel from being taken out into the surrounding community.

Since then, that church leader has been discipling God's people, so that they can do what they saw the preacher dramatically show them on the wall. Go and make disciples.

Back to my question asked at that 'new church' leaders conference. One of the things that Vineyard churches around the world are saying is the following: **Discipleship is not a program. It is not a ministry. It is a lifelong commitment to Jesus, with a lifestyle of going and making disciples**. I couldn't agree more.

I pray that if this book does anything at all, then I hope that it is a call to raise up and nurture faithful disciples of the Shepherd, who commit their lives to authentically follow Him, and who in turn, invite their family, friends, neighbours and work colleagues, into the same relationship that they have with Him.

Questions:

1) Are you a disciple of Jesus? Do you have the desire to do what He is asking of you, and if so, are you equipped to fulfil the call to 'go and make disciples'?

2) If the answer to question one is no, but you have a desire to follow Jesus' instructions, what do you think you should do to further your aims?

CHAPTER 19
THE SHEPHERD AND THE EARTHLY SHEPHERDS AND HIS SERVANTS TODAY

First, we can see from chapters 2 and 3 how an earthly shepherd is supposed to behave, and how the people benefit from such behaviour, but we also see the consequences when the earthly shepherds fail to do what the Shepherd is instructing them to do.

Secondly, I am sad to say that I have friends who have been in full time leadership in the church, doing exactly what the Shepherd has been asking them to do, who have been damaged when the people they shepherd cause chaos and disharmony, and when those who are supposed to oversee and encourage them fail in their obligations. Without fail, the language my friends use is worryingly like each other's statements. It goes something like this – "I love Jesus, but I hate the church".

How can this happen to those the Shepherd calls into service for Him?

Maybe the following can help us to understand both sides of this difficult conundrum.

Tom Wright helpfully says, '**We should preach Good News, that is, Jesus of Nazareth, and not Good Ideas**'.

Preaching and teaching Good News, reveals the Shepherd in all His glory, and it opens the eyes of the hearer in ways that no other form of teaching can.

Preaching and teaching Good Advice, although it may sound very spiritual, does not open people's hearts in the way that the Gospel does. In fact, it can do the opposite and end up bringing more law in to the church, much like the Law that the Pharisees were accused of insisting on when Jesus walked the earth. You may have experienced the following: 'you should do this, you can't do that, you must sit here, you must stand there, you can't marry this person, you can't move to that house, you must agree with the leaders of the church, you can't take communion without going through a course, you are not old enough for baptism, you must dress like this, you must give money to receive blessing, etc. etc. etc'. This list will go on and on, if we let it.

There is nothing wrong and everything right with education and instruction, but is it the Gospel? Are we people after Paul's heart, where he would confront anything that would hinder people made in the image of God, from coming to faith in God's Son, Jesus, or are we more like the Pharisees, who just wanted power over people, so that in their own minds, their leading was secure here on the earth?

The calling to be a leader in the church that Jesus leads, is a very serious calling from the Shepherd. To see the type of people the Shepherd calls, we only need to look at the lives of Peter and Paul. The truth is, that since the fall of mankind in the Garden of Eden, other than Jesus Himself, there has never been a perfect man or woman walking the earth. John Wimber used to say, "Never trust a leader without a limp!" Other church leaders have said something along the lines of, "Church Leaders, please do not sit in judgement over the people of God, or indeed any other person who lives and breathes."

Jesus towards the end of His 'Sermon on the Mount' said this about judging others:

1 'Do not judge, or you too will be judged. 2 For in the same way as you judge others, you will be judged, and with the measure you use, it will be measured to you.

3 'Why do you look at the speck of sawdust in your brother's eye and pay no attention to the plank in your own eye? 4 How can you say to your brother, "Let me take the speck out of your eye," when all the time there is a plank in your own eye? 5 You hypocrite, first take the plank out of your own eye, and then you will see clearly to remove the speck from your brother's eye'. (Matthew 7:1-5 NIV)

I quote my friend Jamie Stilson again from his book, 'The Power of Ugly' (8): **One day my wife started screaming in pain as though I was beating her. We were in an argument, but it was no big deal, except that she kept rolling back and forth as if I was striking her. She informed me it was the plank sticking out of my eye that was assaulting her. I, of course, humbly repented to her saying, "Thank you for pointing out that wonderful truth to me. Not!**

Church leaders need to be humble, honest and self-revealing. Don't listen to those who say that "if we show weakness, others will take advantage of us." This is an enemy strategy, and will lead to difficulty and pain. The Shepherd is looking for those who would 'wash feet' as opposed to those who pretend that they are strong and in control and know everything about everything, and insist upon what they say, goes.

Tom Wright said this: 'We live in a world full of people struggling to be, or at least to appear, strong, in order not to be weak; and we follow a gospel which says that when I am weak, then I am strong. And this gospel is the only thing that brings true healing'.

This is the call on church leadership, for those who are called to be earthly shepherds, reflecting the Shepherd's heart. Father God knows everything about you, even the things that you wish He didn't, and therefore it is foolish to pretend otherwise.

All of this, of course, requires, for their part, that the church honour the servants (The earthly shepherds) that the Shepherd has put in place to protect and serve them. The earthly shepherds are no more or less human than the rest of us, and the church should live its individual and collective life in the same way as them. Humble, honest and self-revealing, and most of all, slow to judge, if at all.

The Shepherd speaks today through His written word and by His Spirit, and I am convinced that He is talking to His church. He calls all of us to a life of following Him and doing the things He spoke about in the Bible, and do what He asks us to do today. We are not called to do what man or woman, however helpful, imaginative and forceful, might insist upon, unless of course, it is in complete agreement with the Bible.

The truth is, everything is about Jesus. It's about His church and His cause. It is His ministry that we are called to. How dare we take anything away from that.

I am reminded of a friend of mine who looked as though she would end up spending a third of the year in the U.S., a third of the year in Canada and a third of the year in the U.K. Her question was, "If this comes about, where will I be able to carry out my ministry?"

It is a language that most of us might recognise today, and it is certainly seen all over the Christian world. 'So and so's ministry', 'big name Christian's ministry', 'mega church's ministry', 'so and so's compassion ministry'. The list is endless. We also have, in the Christian world, different types of 'ministry' that have had their names 'Registered' to protect them. I am not critical of this last part, as I am clear in my own mind that courses like 'The Alpha Course' (12) are Holy Spirit blessed initiatives, and are key to what the Shepherd is doing in the world today. I only ask that we are careful in the way we assess what is done in the name of the Shepherd. All of this got me thinking, and at present, I have concluded that this is the wrong way to look at what we do.

The Shepherd tells us that we don't have a Ministry. It all belongs to Him, and all the glory should go to Him. The truth is that not one of us can heal a broken body, not one of us can save anyone, not one of us has unique insider knowledge of those we minister to, and not one of us can bring peace, hope and joy into people's lives. Only Jesus can do all of this.

The part we must play is to join Jesus in what He is doing, in His ministry. If we must put a name to what He calls us to do, we could say, that doing what the Shepherd tells us to do, is our ministry.

A cry from the heart – please ask the Shepherd what He thinks about what you are saying about what you do. He is gracious and compassionate, and He will answer you in a way that won't crush you.

So, how dare we take away anything from Him. As the leader of Soul Survivor, Mike Pilavachi, once said, "It's all about Jesus. It has always been about Jesus. It will always be about Jesus. There is nothing else."

There are benefits from hearing and responding to the voice of the Shepherd and there are consequences from not doing so.

Questions:

1) Are you a leader with a limp, full of humility, honesty and willing to be self-revealing? Who in your care knows you that well, and is it helpful?

2) Are you preaching Good News, that is, Jesus of Nazareth, or are you into Good Ideas? What would it look like week by week if the voice of Jesus was heard through every word you spoke?

CHAPTER 20
THE SHEPHERD AND YOU THE READER

I have divided this chapter into three main headings, 1) Personal life (character), 2) Calling, and 3) Gifting, which as a practioner of The Gospel, I have found to be the three main areas of our life that the Shepherd speaks into.

1) Personal Life (Character)

Most people I have met, whether they are followers of Jesus or not, desperately need to know that their families, friends, work colleagues are honest, faithful and full of integrity.

Unfortunately, you only need to glimpse at what goes on in the social media to see that we often don't seem to be too good at these things.

This, of course, is not a modern phenomenon.

Throughout history, mankind has lied for his/her own ends, been unfaithful in his/her commitments to family, partners, places of work and nations, and has shown little integrity in his/her dealings with others.

The Old Testament is full of stories about such matters. Just look at the lives of the following and consider the prevailing trend of an unhealthy lifestyle among some of the Bible's greatest people:

Adam, the first man, was a blame shifter who couldn't resist peer pressure. (Genesis 3:12)

Eve, the first woman, couldn't control her appetite. (Genesis 3:6)

Cain, the first born human being, murdered his brother. (Genesis 4:8)

Noah, the last righteous man on earth at the time, was a drunk who slept in the nude. (Genesis 9:20-21)

Abraham, the forefather of faith, let other men walk off with his wife on two different occasions. (Genesis 12 and 20)

Sarah, the most gorgeous woman by popular opinion, let her husband sleep with another woman and then hated her for it. (Genesis 16)

Lot, who lost his father early in life, had a serious problem with choosing the wrong company. (Genesis 19 & 20)

Isaac, who was nearly killed by his father, talked his wife into concealing their marriage. (Genesis 26)

Rebekah, turned out to be a rather manipulative wife. (Genesis 27)

Jacob, who out-wrestled God, was pretty much a pathological deceiver. (Genesis 25, 27, 30)

Rachel, who wrote the book on love at first sight, was a nomadic kleptomaniac. (Genesis 31:19)

Reuben, the pride and firstborn of Jacob, slept with his father's concubine. (Genesis 35:22)

Moses, the humblest man on the face of the earth (Numbers 12:13), had a very serious problem with his temper. (Exodus 2, 32:19; Numbers 20:11)

Miriam, the songwriter, had sibling jealousy and a greed for power. (Numbers 12)

Samson, was hopelessly enmeshed with a disloyal wife—and ended up taking his own life. (Judges 16)

Eli, who ruled over Israel, was a hopelessly incapable father who lost his sons to immorality—and to an untimely death. (1 Samuel 2, 4)

Saul, the first and most powerful king of Israel, was apparently a person with bursts of anger, episodes of deep depression. He committed suicide. (1 Samuel 16, 18, 19, 31)

David, the friend of God, concealed his adultery with a murder. (2 Samuel 11)

Solomon, the wisest man in the world, had 1,000 sexual partners. (1 Kings 11)

With rare exception, all the kings that followed Solomon had major issues in their lives.

Hosea, an incredibly forgiving man, grappled with the pain of a wife who could be described as a nymphomaniac.

The prophets, even as they spoke for God, struggled with impurity, depression, unfaithful spouses and broken families.

Are you feeling encouraged?

Given the state of mankind, how can the Shepherd guide us in all these things?

Jesus' teaching in the 'Sermon on the Mount' is a good place to start. (Matthew 5, 6 & 7)

First, how to be blessed and be a blessing to others.

2 ...He began to teach them. He said:
3   "Blessed are the poor in spirit,
      for theirs is the kingdom of heaven.
4   Blessed are those who mourn,
      for they will be comforted.
5   Blessed are the meek,
      for they will inherit the earth.
6   Blessed are those who hunger and thirst for righteousness,
      for they will be filled.
7   Blessed are the merciful,
      for they will be shown mercy.
8   Blessed are the pure in heart,
      for they will see God.
9   Blessed are the peacemakers,
      for they will be called children of God.
10 Blessed are those who are persecuted because of righteousness,
      for theirs is the kingdom of heaven.

11 "Blessed are you when people insult you, persecute you and falsely say all kinds of evil against you because of me. 12 Rejoice and be glad, because great is your reward in heaven, for in the same way they persecuted the prophets who were before you. (Matthew 5:2-12 NIV)

You can see from these instructions, that the Shepherd identifies that living a life of weakness, mourning, meekness, a desire for righteousness, mercy, purity of heart, peace-making and a life that reflects His earthly life, are some of the key attributes to a life of blessing.

Of course, weakness, mourning, meekness, righteousness, mercy, purity of heart and peace-making are not blessings in themselves, it is God's wonderful response to them that is the blessing. If you look closely, you will see that 'the poor in spirit' *will* be given the Kingdom of

Heaven, 'those who mourn' *will* be comforted, 'the meek' *will* inherit the earth, 'those who hunger' will be filled, 'those who show mercy' *will* be shown mercy, 'the pure in heart *will* see God, 'the peacemakers' *will* be called children of God, and 'those who are persecuted because of the Shepherd' *will* receive the Kingdom of Heaven.

Perhaps a better way of putting this, is that all of it clearly reflects the heart and *will* of God.

How different from the world's ways of doing things?

Secondly, Jesus goes on to talk about being 'Salt and Light' in the world in which we live.

This is about flavouring the society in which we live work and play, and reflecting Him in all that we do and say.

After this, Jesus confirms that "You shall not commit murder", "You shall not commit adultery", (The best teaching that I have ever heard on this subject said, "If you truly love your spouse, it is impossible to commit adultery".) "Do not break your oath", "Turn the other cheek", "Love your enemies", "Give to the needy", "Do not worry", "Do not judge others", and finally Jesus says,

24 Therefore everyone who hears these words of mine and puts them into practice is like a wise man who built his house on the rock. 25 The rain came down, the streams rose, and the winds blew and beat against that house; yet it did not fall, because it had its foundation on the rock. 26 But everyone who hears these words of mine and does not put them into practice is like a foolish man who built his house on sand. 27 The rain came down, the streams rose, and the winds blew and beat against that house, and it fell with a great crash. (Matthew 7:24-27 NIV)

If you desire to have a fulfilled life which is full of integrity, then I would suggest that listening to what the Shepherd says and then doing it, is the way to achieve it.

2) Calling

The call on our lives is first and foremost to a life centred on Jesus, the Good Shepherd, and as a recent Vineyard Churches UK & Ireland conference excitingly pronounced, we are 'Called to **Christ, His Church** and **His Cause**'.

This specific call has been shouted out by the followers of the Shepherd for the last two thousand years or so.

It is a call that should bring peace to all mankind, echoing what the heavenly host proclaimed to the shepherds at the time of Jesus' birth: **Suddenly a great company of the heavenly host appeared with the angel, praising God and saying, "Glory to God in the highest heaven, and on earth peace to those on whom His favour rests".** (Luke 2:13 & 14 NIV)

I leave the reader to question whether this has been the case throughout history?

So, 'Called to **Christ, His Church** and **His Cause**'.

What could this mean?

If you follow Jesus, then you must know that fundamentally

9 … you are a chosen people, a royal priesthood, a holy nation, God's special possession, that you may declare the praises of him who called you out of darkness into his wonderful light. (1 Peter 2:9 NIV)

Or as stated later in the Book of in Revelation,

5 and from Jesus Christ, who is the faithful witness, the firstborn from the dead, and the ruler of the kings of the earth.

To him who loves us and has freed us from our sins by his blood, 6 and has made us to be a kingdom and priests to serve his God

and Father—to him be glory and power for ever and ever! Amen.
(Revelation 1:5 & 6 NIV)

It is clear from the Bible. If you are a follower of Jesus, you are an
intrinsic part of a 'Royal Priesthood'.

How should this work out in our lives?

Even non-believers seem to understand what our job is.

The author, Philip Kerr in the 11ᵗʰ book of his series about his anti-hero,
Bernie Gunther, titled 'The other side of silence', reveals the following:

**Whilst walking around the ruins of the cathedral in Konigsburg
in the mid 1940's, Bernie asks his girlfriend, Irmela to marry him
in the ruins. Irmela says, "We don't even have a priest". Bernie
replies, "Who needs a priest in a Lutheran cathedral? I thought that
was the whole idea of the German Reformation. To abolish priestly
intercession".**

As I have said, it is clear from the Bible that the calling of all followers
of the Shepherd is to fulfil a priestly role.

This is not an argument for abolishing church leadership, neither is it
an argument for not praying for people, nations and creation. It is the
complete opposite.

The church needs earthly shepherds to teach and lead the 'Royal Priests'
of God into a life of prayer. Wouldn't it be wonderful if there were more
people at the church prayer meetings than anything else the church
did? I am reminded of the day that Jo and I went to the Brooklyn
Tabernacle's mid-week prayer meeting. There were over 3,000 people in
the auditorium, kicking up a prayer storm on behalf of the city of New
York. They were just following the Shepherd. Wonderful.

Our friends Jamie and Kim Stilson, the pastors of Cape Vineyard in
Florida, USA, have just turned their church building coffee area into

what they call, 'The Gap'. This is their response to enabling all the people in the church to fulfil the calling on their lives as Kingdom Priests to 'stand in the gap' for their family, friends, neighbours, work colleagues, their city, their State, their country and the world in which they live. Jo and I have had the privilege to be in that room when many 'Kingdom Priests' have been hard at work interceding. It was an awesome experience.

I absolutely believe in the statement, that 'Everybody gets to play'. This amazing saying was penned by John Wimber, the founder of the Vineyard movement, and he would go on afterwards to say, "Now play nicely".

What does this mean for you and me? How does it reflect what the Shepherd is saying?

I have heard all sorts of thoughts about this saying, from those who think that it doesn't mean, 'we all get to do all things', through to those who believe that 'getting to do all things' is exactly what it does mean.

On the cross, just as Jesus gave up His last breath, this happened:

50 And when Jesus had cried out again in a loud voice, he gave up his spirit.

51 At that moment the curtain of the temple was torn in two from top to bottom. (Matthew 27:50-51 NIV)

The curtain mentioned here, is the curtain in the Temple which separates all of mankind, other than the chosen priest for that year, from the very presence of God. This curtain was torn in two, from top to bottom, as a sign from Heaven signifying that through the death of The Messiah, we now have direct access to Father God, without going through an earthly priest.

Paul talks elsewhere in The Bible, that our access to the Father is through the life, death and resurrection of His Son, Jesus, who is the True Shepherd.

14 For he himself is our peace, who has made the two groups one and has destroyed the barrier, the dividing wall of hostility, 15 by setting aside in his flesh the law with its commands and regulations. His purpose was to create in himself one new humanity out of the two, thus making peace, 16 and in one body to reconcile both of them to God through the cross, by which he put to death their hostility. 17 He came and preached peace to you who were far away and peace to those who were near. 18 For through him we both have access to the Father by one Spirit. (Ephesians 2:14-18 NIV)

This statement is either true, or it is part of a story that some followers of Jesus think has been made-up. Looking at how some parts of His church practice, one would think that this is indeed the case.

I don't believe any of this for one second.

I believe passionately that everyone can and does indeed 'get to play'.

This is the calling the Shepherd places on everyone's life. The Shepherd is calling us all to follow Him wherever He leads, to strengthen His church and further His cause.

So whether you are called to lead a church, lead a small group in church, lead a mission at home or overseas, put out chairs in church, provide tea coffee and cakes in church, work in an office, make things in a factory or construct things on a building site, teach in school or university, drive a bus, drive a train or pilot an aircraft, attend school, college or university......the list is endless, I am absolutely certain that the Shepherd is saying to you, you have a calling on your life to follow Him, get involved in His Church and further His Cause wherever you are.

What a privilege.

3) Gifting

There are many wonderful books that have been written and published about Spiritual Gifts, so rather than regurgitating the theories behind them, I want to major here on what the Shepherd is saying to all of us as His followers, with regards to the natural gifts that He gave us as He knitted us together in our mother's womb.

13 For you created my inmost being;

you knit me together in my mother's womb.

14 I praise you because I am fearfully and wonderfully made;

your works are wonderful,

I know that full well. (Psalm 139:13-14 NIV)

As a practioner of The Gospel, I am constantly amazed by the huge variety of natural gifting that God released into the world through us, the people **'made in His image'.** (Genesis 1:27 NIV)

I need to say something here about the 'natural us', before we first decided to follow the Shepherd.

About thirty-five years ago, I was returning from a conference with a bunch of my friends, when one of them asked, "Who wants prayer?" I have always run to the front when prayer is offered, (and why not?) so I shouted out, 'me'.

You need to keep in mind here that most of us wholeheartedly believed in the following scripture:

17 Therefore, if anyone is in Christ, the new creation has come: the old has gone, the new is here! (2 Corinthians 5:17 NIV)

We believed then, and still do today, that everything that existed before we were 'Born Again', needed to die, and indeed when we come to Jesus, we don't come for a better life, more riches or anything else. We come to die.

Much to my surprise, when my friends were praying for me, I saw in my mind's eye, 'little Ronnie' (That is what my mum called me as a boy, because I was named after my dad) walking towards me out of a thick fog. I sensed the Holy Spirit reveal to me that I had divorced myself from myself, and that I needed to know that everything that He knitted together in my mother's womb was good, and He wanted to use all of it for His purposes.

What could this possibly mean, if indeed we are a new creation? Did it have any value now that I was a follower of the Shepherd?

And I thought, "How does Psalm 139 fit in?

1 You have searched me, Lord, and you know me.

2 You know when I sit and when I rise; you perceive my thoughts from afar.

3 You discern my going out and my lying down; you are familiar with all my ways.

4 Before a word is on my tongue you, Lord, know it completely. (Psalm 139:1-4 NIV)

13 For you created my inmost being; you knit me together in my mother's womb.

14 I praise you because I am fearfully and wonderfully made; your works are wonderful; I know that full well.

15 My frame was not hidden from you when I was made in the secret place, when I was woven together in the depths of the earth.

16 Your eyes saw my unformed body; all the days ordained for me were written in your book before one of them came to be.

(Psalm 139:13-16 NIV)

As I have said repeatedly, I am no theologian, but I still wrestle with this subject to this day. I know that I once belonged to sin, but now I have been purchased by the blood of my Saviour, and I now belong to Him. How does this help, if at all?

The only conclusion I can come to is that I know that everything God has made is good (The Bible tells me that), and therefore, as we have a redeeming Saviour (The Bible tells me that), everything that has ever been made can be redeemed. I think this is what the Holy Spirit was revealing to me. (Help, theologians!)

Until somebody can prove to me otherwise (I am very willing to admit that I am wrong if that is the case), I will continue to place in His hands, all the gifting that the Shepherd placed within me since I was knitted together in my mother's womb, and leave it to Him to do whatever He wants to do with it.

The following thoughts must be taken with the caveat that there might be another explanation. However, I leave them with you to decide for yourselves.

When I look around the world and the universe in which we all live, I cannot help but be amazed at the complexity and wonderful detail that goes into everything. Whether it is the way that a single plant is constructed, or a species of animal is uniquely designed, or the way that the sea reacts to the moon, or, etc. etc. etc. The list is endless like all the others contained in this book.

As there are not enough pages in this book to go through every type of gifting, I am going to look at some of them in detail, which, if you then want to look at an individual gift that the Shepherd has given you, you can use the same principles that have driven me to the conclusions that I have come to.

I will be looking at the following areas, without I must confess, much experience in most of them.

Artists, Musicians, Teachers and Designers.

<u>Artists</u>

Throughout history, artists have sought to display what they see and how they see it. Whether it is a wonderful landscape, a unique portrait of a person, a pictorial understanding of a great story, the front cover of a magazine, a cartoon, a cave painting of wild animals, a work of sculpture, a light show or a modern life or abstract depiction, all of them have the individual artist's perceptions and skills deeply etched into them.

I have been told by those that know, that we should not dismiss something just because we don't understand it or even like it. I confess that I have often walked around an art gallery like someone shopping in a supermarket. Just looking for the things that I like and understand. I know that by approaching the art gallery in this manner, I have missed out on some of the world's greatest paintings, sculptures and artwork.

We can all do this when we rush through our busy days. By not seeing and appreciating the wonderful things that God has created, just so we can exist and find delight in our surroundings, we miss out.

Somehow, we need to develop our visual senses just like an artist, to appreciate the world around us. I have heard people marvel at the shape of some of the rain clouds they see, or the colour of the sky when clouds turn to different shades of red, pink or orange, or the colour of the sea, whether it be blue, brown or grey.

All of them wonderful.

However, could we be missing what the artist sees? The clouds as God's way of giving life to the earth, the sunset reflecting the sun given to us by God to keep the earth at just the right temperature to enable life to exist, and the sea, in all its terrible splendour, enabling water to be recycled around the globe. No other element on earth has shaped our civilizations and landscape more than water.

I am reliably informed that 97% of the Earth's water is in our massive oceans. 2% is in lakes, rivers and streams for our consumption. 1% is below the surface.

The amount of water on planet earth has never changed. It has simply changed its location and form over the millennia.

Can we see that?

Gifted artists are still being born today. At the Vineyard church in Dartford, Jo and I have had the privilege of seeing young boys and girls producing some amazing artwork in all its forms. Unfortunately, due to pressure in the modern world to achieve in other areas of their lives, it means that art is eventually relegated to a hobby at best, or forgotten about at worst.

We have family friends whose son, to our mind, has an extraordinary gift at portrait art. Some of the pieces of artwork we have seen of his would not be out of place in a portrait gallery. Today, this young man is very successful in the business world, but oh how we long to see more of his artwork.

How often have you heard or even said yourself, that this or that piece of furniture is handmade? Or that car or boat has been handmade? Or this or that etc. etc.

There is something in this modern world today, where something handmade is looked upon with wonder and awe and which reflects the skill of the maker. The reality is that until modernity, everything that was made, was handmade.

Today, very little is made by a skilful craftsmen's hand, and whilst I understand and accept that machines always reproduce the things that we need or desire in a perfect way and at a cost that we want to pay, there is something deep within us that longs for something original and unique.

Artists can help us in this desire. As we seek to look at the work they provide through their eyes, we can see again our amazing surroundings with new understanding, and appreciate a creative God who gifts people with wonderful insight into the world that He created.

If you are an established artist or just starting out with a dream in your heart, please listen to the Shepherd, who I believe, is calling all the artists that He gifted in their mother's wombs, to release more and more artwork that reflects the creative wonder of His Father in Heaven, for the people of the world to marvel at.

Musicians

I am indebted to the Psalm Drummers (The Psalm Drummers Association Trust info@psalmdrummers.org) who often ask at the beginning of their sessions, "when was the first beat heard on the earth?"

The answer being, the first man Adam's, heartbeat.

If you are like me, when you lay your head on a pillow, very often the first thing you will hear is your heartbeat.

Rhythm has been around that long.

From that rhythm, down the ages has come some wonderful music, written and performed by naturally gifted people, who out of nowhere, have crafted both amazingly complex and stunningly simple delights for us to enjoy and be moved by.

There are remarkably few music notes in the chromatic scale (twelve notes), but from them comes a continuous flow of wonderfully unique music.

The people who write music and lyrics have a wonderful natural gift, which the Shepherd can use to bring the listener to a place where the God of love, is reflected. I have often heard people talk about a song or piece of music that has had them in tears, as they listen with an open heart.

Music and song have always been, and remain today, a strong motivator for the Gospel.

If you are a follower of the Shepherd and you are being used by Him in this area as a song writer or musician, then along with the rest of the church, I applaud you.

If you believe that you have within you the ability to write songs or play an instrument or sing, but you have neither the courage nor opportunity to fulfil this calling on your life, then can I please encourage you to listen to the Shepherd, and start to push doors to see what opens for you.

I believe that we haven't heard the best music or song, because it hasn't been written yet, and we haven't heard the best musician or singer as they haven't been born yet.

John Wimber's wife, Carol, once said that although the church had been blessed by John's songs of intimate worship to Jesus, the church will never hear the best of them, because those were the ones that John sang only to Jesus in his quiet times of worship, and they were never written down or recorded.

I believe that there are many more wonderful songs of praise and worship on song writers hearts, and the world needs to hear them and join in with the whole of creation singing them to the Shepherd.

As a gift, I offer the following set of words for anyone who may be able to put them to music. The only thing I ask is that you let me know how you get on.

BATHED IN GLORY

Flowing from the cross, Jesus You bring splendour,
Where there was shame.
Flowing from the cross, Jesus You bring life,
Where there was death.
You make all things new, Jesus
You make all things new.

Flowing from the cross, Jesus You bring order,
Where chaos reigned.
Flowing from the cross, Jesus You bring freedom,
Where there were chains.
You make all things new, Jesus
You make all things new.
(chorus)
Bathed in glory, no more pain or shame,
Bathed in glory, no more tears or fear,
Bathed in glory, in You, life is full of joy,
Bathed in Glory,
Bathed in glory.
(Ron Warren 2016)

Be blessed by the Shepherd all you song writers and musicians and keep listening to The Holy Spirit as He guides your thinking and writing. I have the courage to call forward into being, that, that doesn't yet exist, unwritten songs of praise and worship to the King of Heaven.

Teachers

Apart from our parents or carers who look after us from birth, surely teachers are the people who have the most profound impact on all our lives.

We should give them honour in society, and respect them for what they do.

This is not a political statement, or perhaps deep down it is, as both our daughter and son-in-law, Charlotte and Andrew are teachers. When I listen to what they say, together with the things other teachers tell me, I don't know how they manage to do what they do for the young people of our country. The workload they have, and the things expected of them, just seems to make their job impossible.

Most teachers are naturally gifted at showing us what things mean, how things work, how to interpret complicated theories, how to compete at sports, how to dance, how to sing, etc.

Teaching is how we all learn.

I can't remember who said it, but I heard on the radio a couple of years ago something that I have never forgotten. This person was talking about the state of our schools with regards to league tables, and he said, 'Surely we want our teachers to do more than just teach. We need them to inspire the next generation'.

That word 'inspire', is I believe, the reason The Shepherd has given teachers the gifts they need, so that each generation can stand on the shoulders of the previous generation, for the good of all mankind.

Be inspired by The Shepherd all you teachers, and go and inspire the next generation on both His and our behalf.

Designers

Design is seen everywhere throughout the universe. Followers of The Shepherd believe that everything that exists has been designed and created by a creator God.

It is everywhere you look.

Whether it is the unique shape of a variety of tree, the different lengths of individual bird species beaks, used for getting into different insect habitations, the various shapes and colours of plant leaves for every conceivable habitat, the different colours and shapes of the bird kingdom, the shape and size of fish species designed for all types of river and sea habitats and different depths of living, the wonderful variation of the animal kingdom, the stars and the planets – the list is endless.

Some say evolution, but I argue, along with many others, a designer, creator God. For me this is not creation versus evolution, but a world view that starts with a creator versus one that has no creator.

Jo and I were flying back from a visit to the States, when as we flew over the western edge of the U.K., I asked The Shepherd, 'How can you possibly know the intimate details of over six billion people who inhabit the earth?'

An impudent question, I know.

The response was unexpected. I heard in my spirit the following answer, 'You still don't understand, do you my son. It's not just the people I know intimately; I know every blade of grass down there'.

I think this was The Shepherd confirming to me in a roundabout way what He spoke to His followers in the days when He walked on the earth, **and even the very hairs of your head are all numbered.** (Matthew 10:30 NIV)

I haven't asked that question since! (You may well say, very wise.)

If, like the Bible says, **we are made in His image,** (Genesis 1:27 NIV) is it any wonder that there are so many designers in the world?

Everything we see, use and sometimes eat, (certainly the recipes and packaging, food comes in) has been designed by someone.

The dwellings we live in, the cars that we drive, the roads that we drive on, buses, trains and airplanes we travel in, cinemas, shopping centres and cities we visit, books that we read, the seats that we sit on, beds that we sleep in – everything designed by a designer.

We would almost certainly argue between ourselves what we think is good and bad design, and what we like and dislike, and this will always be a subjective view of things. However, this does not mean that they were not designed.

Every designer I have come across, is generally proud of what they have designed, and I believe rightly so.

As a reflection of a designer, creator God, The Shepherd will use this gift distributed among mankind, to glorify His Father in Heaven.

As an example, I have heard it said by some that the great cathedrals of the world were designed and built for the glory of the architect/builder and those who funded the work. I don't believe this at all. I am sure that The Shepherd was calling the designers, builders and funders to build something here on the earth that would glorify His Father in Heaven.

So, if you are a designer reading this, can I encourage you to listen to what The Shepherd is saying to you and hear how He wants you to use your design creativity to glorify His Father in Heaven?

The Shepherd and You the Reader - Conclusion

When I first started work, I was an office boy in an architect's office in London. The plan was for my employer to gradually introduce me to a drawing board, so that I could begin learning how things worked in the real world. After six months of serving tea and biscuits together with delivering the post around the office, I remember asking my dad about how much longer did he think that I should be an office boy?

I have not forgotten my dad's response to my question. He said that 'nobody goes to work to deliberately do a bad job'. To put this response into context, my dad was a self-employed carpenter and joiner, and if he damaged anything he was working on, maybe a door, or worktop, or roof structure, and it proved to be his fault, the cost of replacing the damaged items was deducted from his pay. He was so good at his trade, that he could boast that he never had a deduction from his pay for all the time that he worked.

In my dad's answer to my question, he was really saying 'do what you are being paid to do today, and do it to your best ability, without making a fuss. After this conversation, and to my mind, I became the best provider of tea and deliverer of post that the office had ever known.

I remember that about two weeks later, I was given a drawing board, and then I started to learn how to design houses.

Now let me point you to your creator.

26 Then God said, 'Let us make mankind in our image, in our likeness, so that they may rule over the fish in the sea and the birds in the sky, over the livestock and all the wild animals, and over all the creatures that move along the ground.'

27 So God created mankind in his own image, in the image of God, he created them; male and female he created them.

(Genesis 1:26-27 NIV)

God sees all that He has made, and it is very good.

To subdue an unruly world, and further the Kingdom of God, the world needs the best at everything we do.

It needs the best………………………

academics, architects, actors, airmen and women, artists, aunts, authors, brothers, builders, bus drivers, carpenters, children, church leaders, conductors, dads, dentists, doctors, drivers, daughters, electricians, engineers, factory workers, farmers, fire officers, gardeners, grandparents, guards, hairdressers, iron workers, judges, kiln workers, knife sharpeners, knitters, librarians, lovers, magistrates, managers, models, mums, musicians, nurses, opera singers, parents, plasterers, police officers, politicians, plumbers, prison warders, quarry workers, Queen's Counsellors, quilters, railway workers, sailors, secretaries, shopkeepers, singers, sisters, soldiers, solicitors, sons, sportsmen and women, surgeons, taxi drivers, teachers, traffic wardens, train drivers, T V presenters, uncles, upholsterers, ushers, varnishers, vets, welders, x-ray technicians, yard workers, yoga teachers, youth workers, zoo keepers, etc.

Are you created to be anyone mentioned in this short list, or any other profession, trade or relationship that has not been mentioned?

Because the answer to this question is surely yes, I must tell you that The Shepherd is for you and not against you. His desire is to help you do all that you are called to do with as much honesty and integrity that you can muster.

This is not about being perfect, for as we have seen, other than Jesus, no human being is perfect. It is about 'The Shepherd Speaks… Do you hear Him?'

Questions:

Personal Life:

Do you want to have a fulfilled life full of integrity and passion?

If the answer is yes, then listen to what The Shepherd says and do what He says.

Calling:

Do you know what the calling on your life is?

If the answer is yes, are you following that call?

If the answer is no, then I encourage you to ask The Shepherd for guidance.

Gifting:

Are you secure in the natural gifting that The Shepherd has built into you?

If not, please ask for confirmation from the One who created you.

CHAPTER 21
FINAL THOUGHTS

The following song lyrics from the band 'Casting Crowns', I believe, shows the consequences of when the voice of The Shepherd is ignored, and all the people made in His image who do not know Him, are lost and far away from the security that Jesus provides through His life, death and resurrection.

But if we are the body
Why aren't His arms reaching?
Why aren't His hands healing?
Why aren't His words teaching?

And if we are the body
Why aren't His feet going?
Why is His love not showing them?
There is a way?
(Casting Crowns – 'If we are the body) (9)

How different the world would look if those who are followers of Jesus would listen to Him and do exactly what Mary told the servants to do over two thousand years ago – 'Whatever He tells you to do, do it'.

What is The Shepherd saying today?

If you are a scientist, or someone who is beginning to understand how creation works; if you are a church leader; if you are a song writer, a musician, or an artist; if you are a craftsman, a designer, a secretary, or a banker; if you are a mother, a father, a brother, a sister, an aunt, or an uncle; if you are at school or college or university; if you clean the roads, remove rubbish, or clean drains; if you are a soldier, sailor, or airman; if you are just an 'ordinary' person trying to get through life; this is what I sense The Shepherd would say to you:

Do everything you do as worship to me, being honest, faithful and true, and whenever you can, and at every opportunity I give you, listen to my voice and do whatever I ask you to do, in the power of the Holy Spirit, always giving praise and honour to your Father in heaven. That is all that I ask of you, and never forget My promise that I will be with you until the end of time.

The Saviour and Lord of all creation sits at the right hand of The Father right now, speaking to Him about every situation and all things, good or bad, happening today in the whole of the universe, which includes amazingly, you and me, and He is asking His body here on the earth to continue His earthly ministry, thus fulfilling His commands and the prophetic words spoken about Him by the prophet Isaiah -

The Spirit of the Sovereign Lord is on me, because the Lord has anointed me to proclaim good news to the poor. He has sent me to bind up the broken-hearted, to proclaim freedom for the captives and release from darkness for the prisoners, to proclaim the year of the Lord's favour and the day of vengeance of our God, to comfort all who mourn, and provide for those who grieve in Zion – bestow on them a crown of beauty instead of ashes, the oil of joy instead of mourning, and a garment of praise instead of a spirit of despair. (Isaiah 61:1-3 N I V)

Jesus quoted the first part of this prophecy in the synagogue in Nazareth, confirming to those who would listen, the essence of His ministry. These words also describe the very heart of His ministry that He passed on to His church to fulfil, until He returns.

There are countless thousands of followers of The Shepherd working across the globe today, listening and fulfilling the commands of The Shepherd, and they are doing wonderful, marvellous and essential work extending the Kingdom of God. In their wake, millions of people are being set free from all kinds of life difficulties, and we should pray for these followers of Jesus and give thanks to God for their obedience and courage.

So, a final, final thought.

let's look at the three major responses that The Shepherd is looking for in His followers, based upon just two of His people, Moses and Gideon, who were written about in the Old Testament.

FIRST, BE REAL.

It's comforting to me that when God looks for someone to use, He looks for reality in their lives, and doesn't often look for someone doing heroic things. He found **Moses** in the desert – a fugitive from justice. (Exodus 2, 3 & 4) and He found **Gideon** at the bottom of a winepress. (Judges 6 & 7)

When God wants to turn a nobody into a somebody, he takes the nobody just as they are. This is such good news for you and me.

SECOND, BE OBEDIENT

Let's take Moses first. After the burning bush incident, Moses kept on saying to God, 'who am I that You would use me?'. Having said this to God, he is eventually obedient to the call, and does exactly what God had told him to do.

Now for Gideon. He clearly wasn't the best example of someone responding to God quickly. He hesitated before answering God's call. He feared that his own limitations would prevent God from working. But he was obedient.

Obedience is all that our Father in heaven wants from us.

THIRD, GET OUT OF GOD'S WAY

When God takes a nobody, and turns them into a somebody, that nobody must learn how to get out of God's way. They must be real, and they must be obedient, but there comes a time when the individual needs to put down their natural abilities, step aside and let God work through them.

There is much more to do, and my guess is that, right now you are being called to listen to The Shepherd, and with all the courage and hope that you can muster, I beg you, please do what He asks you to do.

There are benefits from hearing and responding to the voice of the Shepherd and there are consequences from not doing so.

APPENDIX 1

'THE I AM SAYINGS OF THE SHEPHERD'

In Matthew 16:13-16 Jesus first asks the disciples, **'Who do people say that I am?'** and then He asks them, **'Who do you say that I am?'** If we can respond to the same questions Jesus asks today, our answers will reveal the truth about our relationship with Him, our trust in Him, and our level of faith in Him.

Jesus knows the answers to the 'I AM' questions, and we can find them in John's gospel.

These seven 'I AM' sayings reflect what God said to Moses back in Exodus:

13 Moses said to God, 'Suppose I go to the Israelites and say to them, "The God of your fathers has sent me to you," and they ask me, "What is his name?" Then what shall I tell them?'

14 God said to Moses, 'I am who I am. This is what you are to say to the Israelites: "I am has sent me to you".
(Exodus 3:13-14 NIV)

The seven *'I AM'* statements are:

Then Jesus declared, 'I am the bread of life. Whoever comes to me will never go hungry, and whoever believes in me will never be thirsty'. (John 6:35 NIV)

We find this statement the day after the miraculous story of the feeding of over 5,000 people, on the mountainside near the Sea of Galilee.

When Jesus speaks of being the bread of life, He understands that there is a hunger and an appetite deep down in all of mankind. However, it is easy to see from scripture that the people had confused physical bread for this deeper one. **'You are looking for me'** Jesus said in John 6:26 (NIV) **'not because you saw the signs I performed but because you ate the loaves and had your fill'**. The Shepherd is saying, 'You didn't see the signs and say, "how do we follow them to find the living bread?" You have come, because you want to see another miracle. You are obsessed with them'.

It is clear from this verse that we need to open our spiritual eyes to the deeper things of God, so that we can experience, apart from the physical things we crave for in the material world, the real food, which will free us from real hunger. The crowd didn't understand, so Jesus rebukes them.

You would think that the lesson would have been learnt. Look what happens next. **'So, they asked him, "What sign then will you give that we may see it and believe you? What will you do?'** (John 6:30 NIV) Mankind is so fickle. Jesus, the day before, had fed at least 5,000 people with five loaves and two fish. (Have you seen the size of the small fish from that area?) Not only that, but there seemed to be lots left over. The crowd, which had followed Him across the lake, had witnessed this miracle and were presumably full. Can you imagine them saying something like, 'That was impressive, give us another one?' They go on to say, **our ancestors ate the manna in the wilderness; as it is written: 'He gave them bread from heaven to eat.'** (John 6:31 NIV) It is almost like them saying, 'What you did was impressive, but look at what was provided for our forefathers not once, but every day for forty years'.

Now we get to the truth of what Jesus is saying. Jesus responds to the people in the following way, **'Very truly I tell you, it is not Moses who has given you the bread from heaven, but it is my Father who gives** you the true bread from heaven. For the bread of God is the bread that comes down from heaven and gives life to the world'. (John 6:32-33 NIV)

Such fickle people. Now they want it. 'Sir,' they said, 'always give us this bread'. (John 6:34 NIV)

Jesus responds to them, 'I am the bread of life. Whoever comes to me will never go hungry, and whoever believes in me will never be thirsty'. (John 6:35 NIV)

The manna miraculously supplied by God for His people in the wilderness, was only good for the day it was given. It was not designed for the following day. The manna satisfied their hunger, but it was more than that. It was a sign that pointed to someone greater, the Lord Jesus, who said, 'I am the bread of life. He who comes to Me will never go hungry', which was the complete opposite to the bread given in the wilderness, and He goes on to say, 'and he who believes in Me will never be thirsty'. The second part of this statement is followed up below.

Jesus is talking about Himself, someone much richer and more satisfying than bread. This is more than just accepting Jesus Christ into our hearts and following Him, although that is critical for life. The Shepherd is talking about all of us feeding on Him every day, so that we can participate in His wonderful, never ending, provision.

Concerning the last part of Jesus' statement about never being thirsty, we don't need to look further than the story of when He met the woman of Samaria, as recorded in John chapter 4.

He talked to the woman in the same terms about water quenching her thirst. He was travelling from Judea up to Galilee, and when he was in Samaria He came across this lady at the well. I can't think that this was an accident!

Jesus asked the woman for some water, and this is how the conversation proceeds:

7 When a Samaritan woman came to draw water, Jesus said to her, "Will you give me a drink?" 8 (His disciples had gone into the town to buy food.)

9 The Samaritan woman said to him, "You are a Jew and I am a Samaritan woman. How can you ask me for a drink?" (For Jews do not associate with Samaritans.)

10 Jesus answered her, "If you knew the gift of God and who it is that asks you for a drink, you would have asked him, and he would have given you living water."

11 "Sir," the woman said, "you have nothing to draw with and the well is deep. Where can you get this living water? 12 Are you greater than our father Jacob, who gave us the well and drank from it himself, as did also his sons and his livestock?"

13 Jesus answered, "Everyone who drinks this water will be thirsty again, 14 but whoever drinks the water I give them will never thirst. Indeed, the water I give them will become in them a spring of water welling up to eternal life." (John 4:7-14 NIV)

Here is the woman's response:

'Sir, give me this water so that I won't get thirsty and have to keep coming here to draw water'. (John 4:15 NIV)

Like the statement about natural bread, Jesus sees in this woman a thirst which is more than just about drawing water from a well. This thirst is something deep in her very being. Jesus tells her that she can go on drinking the water from the well, but if that is all she does, she will be thirsty again very soon. To satisfy her thirst, she should drink from Him, then she would never thirst again.

None of what Jesus says is against eating and drinking in the natural world. We need food and drink to survive. The challenge here, for all of us, is to seek solutions for the world's hungry and their need for clean drinking water.

Jesus is delivering spiritual truths. Just as we share in the spiritual experience of the breaking of bread and drinking wine at Holy Communion, so we eat and drink His provision, and as we do, His promise is that we will never go spiritually hungry or thirsty again.

"When Jesus spoke again to the people, he said, 'I am the light of the world. Whoever follows me will never walk in darkness, but will have the light of life." (John 8:12 NIV)

This statement comes in the Temple Courts at the end of the story of the woman caught in adultery.

To both the woman and her accusers, Jesus is shining the light of truth into their hearts. His purpose is to liberate them all if they would only respond to Him, because what He is showing them is the light of life, not the light of condemnation. Only the light of life will bring them out of the darkness they are in, into life.

The place in the Bible where this is supported is in the book of Job. Job is speaking, and he says of God,

He reveals the deep things of darkness and brings utter darkness into the light. (Job 12:22 NIV)

Jesus knows that hidden secret things are dangerous. Sins hidden in the dark have no boundaries; there is nothing to hem them in because they are surrounded by the dark. Jesus knows that such sins, if left there, can expand, and eventually cause the havoc that the enemy has planted them for, in the first place.

How many times have we seen the good and powerful brought low because of something they have done in the dark?

Moses says in his Psalm 90 verse 8 **'You have set our iniquities before you, our secret sins in the light of your presence'.** (NIV)

God exposes sin not to accuse, humiliate, or condemn. He does it to liberate, cleanse and to empower. For health, God knows that sin must be exposed. In 1 John 1:9, we read, **if we confess our sins, he is faithful and just and will forgive us our sins and purify us from all unrighteousness.** (NIV)

The only way to overcome sin is to speak it out through the mouth. By doing this, it is brought out of the dark, and brought into the light.

This is the foundation of Jesus' statement. His promise is that whoever follows Him will never fear the dark. For each one, the light of heaven will remain with them, and the darkness will never overcome it.

Have you ever tried to block out the light of the sun?

*"**I am the gate**; whoever enters through me will be saved. They will come in and go out, and find pasture."* (John 10:9 NIV)

Other than the truth of this verse, I can't help but think that Jesus makes this statement, because it looked for all to see, that the Pharisees regarded themselves as the gatekeepers of God's kingdom. They seemed determined to be the ones who decided who would be allowed in and who would be rejected.

The Pharisees had no real, living experience of God, much less a relationship with Him. They set themselves up as the chief and only authority in the laws of God. They made up and imposed human rules and heavy burdens on the people, which was an earthly programme that could not possibly offer life, hope or inner peace.

The only interest they had was their own success. Their idea seemed to be that if you conformed to their rules, you would please God and therefore satisfy their requirements, and if you satisfied their requirements, you would satisfy God. To my mind, they seemed determined to be the arbiters of the people's standing before God, and all of it based on which people belonged to them.

Jesus is clear. He is the gate, and nobody else has the authority or power to grant access, and what's more, He will never delegate this authority and power to anyone or anything. There are no side doors, no back doors, and especially, no secret doors. We only get into heaven through Jesus. He is Lord.

"I am the good shepherd. The good shepherd lays down his life for the sheep." (John 10:11 NIV)

I hope that this book covers this statement in as much detail as you might need?

"Jesus said to her, 'I am the resurrection and the life. The one who believes in me will live, even though they die." (John 11:25 NIV)

This statement comes in the passage talking about the resurrection of Jesus' friend, Lazarus.

Jesus arrives in Bethany to be greeted by Martha. **'Lord,' Martha said to Jesus, 'if you had been here, my brother would not have died'.** (John 11:21 NIV)

The thing to note here is that Martha's words are in the past tense. We can't be too critical of Martha, because which one of us would have said anything different?

Martha's sister Mary says the same thing, **When Mary reached the place where Jesus was and saw him, she fell at his feet and said, 'Lord, if you had been here, my brother would not have died'.** (John 11:32 NIV)

There is that one word again – 'if'. How many of us have lived in the place of 'if'?

In the depth of all the heartache, Jesus responds:

23 Jesus said to her, "Your brother will rise again."

24 Martha answered, "I know he will rise again in the resurrection at the last day". (John 11:23-24 NIV)

You can sense that Martha can only see Jesus' comments as a future promise. It doesn't seem to give her any comfort in her distress. Her only brother, presumably the bread winner in the family, is dead. What are they to do? Can you see the battle going on here?

Martha and Mary believe in the power of Jesus in the past, and they believe in the power of Jesus in the future. They have no problem with any of that, but what about now? In their despair, they miss the most important thing about Jesus. In the very next verse, Jesus looks at Martha, almost certainly with compassion in His heart, and says to her,

25 "I am the resurrection and the life. The one who believes in me will live, even though they die; 26 and whoever lives by believing in me will never die. Do you believe this?" (John 11:25-26 NIV)

Both Martha and Mary have seen all that Jesus had done in the past. Their cry is, 'If only you had been here?' Martha in this case, doesn't seem to be consoled by what Jesus will do in the future.

During the turmoil of these emotions, Jesus reveals to them the truth of who He is. The very thing that they needed right then. Jesus says, "I AM".

Not in the past, not in the future, but right now. Imagine the joy in the household.

"Jesus answered, 'I am the way and the truth and the life. No one comes to the Father except through me." (John 14:6 NIV)

This statement is probably the most difficult and controversial one Jesus ever made in history. You and I, before knowing Him, might think that it would be far more reasonable if He had said, "I am a way, I am a truth, I am a life; you may come to the Father through Me," but no. Jesus is clear about who He is. He is the only way in which we may come to God.

In this statement, Jesus reveals Himself with four truths: "I am the way; I am the truth; I am the life," and "no one comes to the Father except through me."

'THE WAY' - 'A way' on a sign board indicates a journey between two points in geography. In the Christian life, the journey is not to a place but to a person. Jesus is pointing to the Father. The objective of the journey Jesus talks about is reconciliation to God.

'THE TRUTH' – What is this truth Jesus is talking about? If you study the life of Jesus, you will find that He is the truth about God. At the Last Supper, Philip has this conversation with Jesus:

7 If you really know me, you will know my Father as well. From now on, you do know him and have seen him."

8 Philip said, "Lord, show us the Father and that will be enough for us."

9 Jesus answered: "Don't you know me, Philip, even after I have been among you such a long time? Anyone who has seen me has seen the Father. How can you say, 'Show us the Father'? (John 14:7-9 NIV)

If you are as inquisitive as me, the question that comes to mind is, what did the disciples of Jesus see? I like to think that they saw in Jesus, a man as God created man to be.

Genesis 1:26-27 emphasizes four times that God created us in His image. For God, the purpose of mankind before the fall, was to share in the relationship that the Father, Son and Holy Spirit had, and to demonstrate in the way they lived and behaved, what God is like. Jesus lived as a man here on the earth in complete union with His Father, in utter obedience to Him, with a complete dependence on Him and an overwhelming love for Him. When Philip looks at Jesus, he sees God in action.

It was apparently clear that all the miracles and teaching of Jesus were His Father working through Him. As a man on the earth, the relationship Jesus had with His Father, was the same relationship that Jesus says we can have with Him today.

'THE LIFE' – From the above notes we can see that Jesus is the way to God, and that He is the truth about God, but there is surely something missing. What was it that Adam and Eve lost in the Garden of Eden? After they ate the forbidden fruit, God banished them from the garden, and they lost the intimate relationship they had with God. They did not die physically, but they did lose the life that God had made them for, when He breathed life into them. It is this life that Jesus is talking about.

The final words in the verse repeat again, that only He can give access to our heavenly Father.

"I am the true vine, and my Father is the gardener." (John 15:1 NIV)

This is the seventh and final "I Am" statement in John's gospel. What could it mean?

If you study the Bible you will find that the vine is used throughout the scriptures to represent Israel, the people of God. In Psalm 80:8, you will find that Israel is called the vine that was brought out of Egypt. **'You transplanted a vine from Egypt; you drove out the nations and planted it.'** (NIV)

In Isaiah 5, known as 'The Song of the Vineyard', we see Israel as a corrupted vine. Jeremiah 2:21 makes the same connection of Israel as the corrupt vine. *'I had planted you like a choice vine of sound and reliable stock. How then did you turn against me into a corrupt, wild vine?'* (NIV)

In chapters 15, 17, and 19 of the book of Ezekiel, you will also see Israel called the vine.

In this statement, Jesus is identifying himself as Israel. Unlike the Israel revealed above, He is saying, He is the true Israel. Jesus is teaching His followers that Israel, as God created it to be, had failed on every level. The prophets Isaiah, Jeremiah and Ezekiel had all made this point.

The good news is that it is not the end of God's plan for the world He created, or for the people made in His image. In Jesus we find success, where Israel had failed.

Jesus is absolutely everything that God desired.

The historical nation of Israel, described as a vine, has been replaced by Jesus, who is, as He states, the true vine.

The second part of this statement sees the Father described as the expert gardener who is cultivating this relationship. The Father who planted and cultivated the vine relationship with Israel, is now tending this relationship with Jesus as the true vine.

1 'I am the true vine, and my Father is the gardener. 2 He cuts off every branch in me that bears no fruit, while every branch that does bear fruit he prunes so that it will be even more fruitful'. (John 15:1-2 NIV)

It seems clear to me that there can be no misunderstanding of who a follower of the Shepherd is and who is not. We don't need to ask. The evidence of who belongs to Jesus and who doesn't is fruitfulness.

It is not possible to remain in relationship with Jesus and not bear fruit!

Jesus is talking about a relationship of intimacy. Jesus lives and forever remains in us the same way that we live and remain in Him. It is clear in the picture revealed in this illustration. It is not possible for a branch to bear fruit by itself. The branch must be connected to, and live in the vine. The job of the branch is to get its sustenance from the vine, and the job of the vine is to produce fruit through its branches.

There is only one reason a branch bears fruit. It is because it is connected to the vine.

Fruitfulness in the lives of followers of The Shepherd is unbelievably important for two reasons.

Firstly, our Father in Heaven is glorified by our fruitfulness. We exist for God's glory. Jesus came to show the glory of God to the world, and following in His footsteps, we are to do the same through fruitfulness.

Secondly, that through our fruitfulness, we prove to a hurting world that we are followers of Jesus. It is not possible to be a follower of Jesus and not show more and more fruit.

Here is the truth of what Jesus says, when we remain in Him, we will have His Spirit in our hearts with the inevitable consequence of bearing fruit. The promise of The Father is that He will prune us, so that we can be more fruitful. Hallelujah.

If these thoughts turn you to prayer, then I suggest a good way to start would be to use the words of the well-known vineyard song by Danny Daniels, 'You are the vine, we are the branches'...........

And we'll go in Your love
And we'll go in Your name
That the world will surely know
That You have power
To heal and to save
You are the vine
We are the branches
Keep us abiding in You

So, there you have it. To clarify for those who would listen, Jesus has a conversation with the Pharisees, ending with the following discourse, putting all the above into context:

52 At this they exclaimed, 'Now we know that you are demon-possessed! Abraham died and so did the prophets, yet you say that whoever obeys your word will never taste death. 53 Are you greater than our father Abraham? He died, and so did the prophets. Who do you think you are?'

54 Jesus replied, 'If I glorify myself, my glory means nothing. My Father, whom you claim as your God, is the one who glorifies me. 55 Though you do not know him, I know him. If I said I did not, I would be a liar like you, but I do know him and obey his word. 56 Your father Abraham rejoiced at the thought of seeing my day; he saw it and was glad.'

57 'You are not yet fifty years old,' they said to him, 'and you have seen Abraham!'

58 'Very truly I tell you,' Jesus answered, 'before Abraham was born, I am!' 59 At this, they picked up stones to stone him, but Jesus hid himself, slipping away from the temple grounds.
(John 8:52-59 NIV)

C. S. Lewis, in his book 'Mere Christianity' (19) said the following about The Shepherd, as revealed in His *'I AM'* statements:

A man who was merely a man and said the sort of things Jesus said would not be a great moral teacher. He would either be a lunatic -- on the level with a man who said he was a poached egg -- or else he would be the Devil of Hell.

You must make your choice.

Either this man was, and is, the Son of God: or else a madman or something worse. You can shut him up for a fool, you can spit at Him and kill Him as a demon; or you can fall at His feet and call Him Lord and God. But let us not come with some patronising nonsense about Him being a great human teacher. He has not left that open to us. He did not intend to.

There is nothing more to say.

APPENDIX 2

'THE SHEPHERD AND THE POOR AND NEEDY'

All they asked was that we should continue to remember the poor, the very thing I had been eager to do all along. (Galatians 2:10 NIV)

The only additional thing they asked was that we remember the poor, and I was already eager to do that. (Galatians 2:10 The Message)

I have shown below just three of the many scriptures from a total of over one hundred and ten, that appear in the Old Testament, relating to the poor and the needy. These will give you a flavour of what The Shepherd feels about how His people, the church, should approach people who have far less than those who have plenty.

Remember too, that their names are not 'the poor'. Each one has a name, and each one is cherished in Heaven for who they are, not for the situation they find themselves in.

Whoever oppresses the *poor* shows contempt for their Maker, but whoever is kind to the *needy* honours God. (Proverbs 14:31 NIV)

Whoever is kind to the *poor* lends to the Lord, and he will reward them for what they have done. (Proverbs 19:17 NIV)

He defended the cause of the *poor* and *needy*, and so all went well. Is that not what it means to know me?' declares the Lord. (Jeremiah 22:16 NIV) (Italics are mine)

The Shepherd says something very difficult to hear, for those who do not listen. Please read the following with fear and trembling, because it is the heart of The Shepherd:

I can't stand your religious meetings. I'm fed up with your conferences and conventions.

I want nothing to do with your religion projects, your pretentious slogans and goals.

I'm sick of your fund-raising schemes, your public relations and image making.

I've had all I can take of your noisy ego-music. When was the last time you sang to me?

Do you know what I want?

I want justice—oceans of it.

I want fairness—rivers of it.

That's what I want. That's all I want.

(Amos 5:21-24 The Message)

Why all this angst from a loving Father?

It is because God's people, Israel, had forgotten the calling of The Shepherd.

They had turned justice into bitterness, and cast fairness out of the door.

They hated those who upheld justice in the courts, and they detested those who told the truth.

They oppressed the innocent, and took bribes and deprived the poor of justice in the courts.

I am reminded of some words that two of The Shepherd's followers today have cried out in the recent past.

The first came from the astonishing servant of the King, Jackie Pullinger MBE. Jackie is a British Protestant Christian missionary in Hong Kong and she is founder of the St. Stephen's Society. (17).

On hearing about the visitation of the Holy Spirit at the Airport Church in Toronto, Canada, Jackie was heard to have said, "Now my brothers and sisters will come to help us." Later, she said, "They have spent loads of money flying back and forth to Toronto from all over the world to receive blessing, and all they have done with it is take it back to their home churches, and kept it there for themselves." Of course, this wasn't the whole story, as some amazing things were birthed in Toronto, and many people were released by the Shepherd to serve Him all over the world, and I am sure that Jackie would agree with this. However, I sense that the essence of what this servant of the Living God said, is – Be very careful with what The Shepherd gives you. It is not just for you; it is for those who don't know Jesus as their Saviour. It is for the poor and needy, for the disadvantaged and for the broken and damaged individuals, who struggle just to live in this very materialistic and dangerous world.

In an article Jackie wrote for the Vineyard Churches U K & Ireland, which can be found in full on the Vineyard website, she said the following:

<u>'You can do nothing on your own'</u>

Run the race marked out for you. You can't run my race, and I will not run yours. Don't compare yours with anyone's. If you have started ministering with the unlovely, if you have started ministering

with the poor, and they haven't come to the Lord, and you haven't seen any numbers you can count, it doesn't matter. Just be faithful in loving that one. Don't compare yourself with anyone else. Give yourself fully to the work of the Lord, because you know your labour in the Lord is not in vain.

'It doesn't matter if you see results or not'

It doesn't matter if you see results or not. You mustn't be proud of yourself because there are results or depressed because there aren't. Neither of these is an accurate reflection of your ministry. You know your labour in the Lord is not in vain, so you do it anyway. Is that not what Jesus did for us? Did he not die before we said, "Thank you"? He didn't decide to die when we put up our hand to accept him. He died anyway, and that's how we are to minister to the poor. We give up our lives whether they accept Christ as Saviour or not. If they swear at us, we still love them.

That's the gospel. That's the privilege of this particular ministry. Therefore, faint ye not. Your actions will bear fruit that is uncountable.

Minister to each one as if he is the only one in the world for whom Jesus died.

Jackie started this article in such a way, that will encourage us to listen to The Shepherd, and do what He asks us to do:

God, in his mercy, rescues the poor, saves them, and gives them new life.

I'm convinced that if you want an evangelism explosion, if you want to reach the world in the quickest possible time so Jesus can come back, you must go for the poor.

Marvellous! Wonderful! Thank you, Jackie.

The second came from Pastor Pete Cunningham, one of the founders of the housing charity, 'Green Pastures'. (18) I remember the first time I met Pastor Pete in Dartford. He talked about his desire to end, completely, homelessness in his home town of Southport, North West England.

This is part of what he says on their website:

Our first resident, a single mother aged 21, had been living in one room with her baby. What a joy it was to be able to help her and to fulfil God's word. In Galatians 2:10 Paul writes: 'They desire only that we should remember the poor: the very thing that I was also eager to do.' It had appeared to us that the 21st Century church was not so eager to help the poor as the early church had been. Perhaps through Green Pastures we shall be able to encourage that eagerness to return. In 1995 we started our first partnership outside Southport and started housing the homeless in Manchester. Today we have partners all over the UK who are housing hundreds of formerly homeless people.

We dream of homelessness ending in the UK. Through our partners we aim to soon be housing more than 1,000 people and we dream of every church in the UK having one house to house the homeless. That would mean an additional 100,000 people would be housed and cared for.

Now, according to the Green Pastures website in late 2017, there are just 48 churches nationwide, who are identified as 'Partners' with Green Pastures. If we are to take the call of The Shepherd seriously, we should be seeing more and more church communities putting their shoulder to this wheel. I know from my son-in-law, Phil Conn, who heads-up a homeless work in the North East of England, that there are many Christian charities throughout the land, following the Shepherd's calling on homelessness. Our prayer must be, Lord, let there be more. Remember, that resources will follow a Godly vision.

Is there any one of us, who wouldn't want to sleep in a safe, warm bed?

It is the heart of The Shepherd. It is our job description.

Real religion, the kind that passes muster before God the Father, is this: Reach out to the homeless and loveless in their plight, and guard against corruption from the godless world. (James 1:27 The Message)

John Wimber was fond of asking the following two questions: **'What business are you in?'**, and **'How's business?**

The Shepherd is asking the same two questions today. To every one of His followers, are you listening?

BIBLIOGRAPHY

1 – Scripture quotations identified NIV are taken from *The Holy Bible, New International Version*. Biblica and Hodder & Stoughton, 1979, 1984, 2011.

2 – Urquhart, Colin. *The Truth version of the Bible*. Horsham, England. Kingdom Faith, 2011

3 – Henry, Matthew. *Commentary on the whole Bible*. Nashville, TN. Thomas Nelson Inc., 2003.

4 – White, John. *The Fight*. Downers Grove, IL. Inter Varsity Press, 1976.

5 – Wright, Nicholas Thomas. *John for Everyone – Part One*. London, England. SPCK, 2002.

6 – Vineyard Churches USA. *Cutting Edge*. (vol. 14 no.2)

7 – Peterson, Eugene. *Reversed Thunder*. Reprinted edition. San Francisco, CA. Harper San Francisco, 1991.

8 – Stilson, Jamie J. *The Power of Ugly*. Woodinville, WA. Harmon Press, 2010.

9 – Casting Crowns. *'If we are the Body'* (Song)

10 - *The N I V Study Bible*. Biblica and Hodder & Stoughton, 2015.

11 - Packer, J I. *Keeping in Step with the Spirit: Finding Fullness in Our Walk with God*. Ada, MI. Baker Books, 1984, 2005.

12 - *The Alpha Course*. Alpha HQ, Brompton Road, London, SW7 1JA.

13 - Doherty, Kevin. *Villa Normandie*. London, England. Endeavour Press Ltd., 2015.

14 - Peterson, Eugene H. *The Message*. First edition. Carol Stream, IL. NavPress, 2003.

15 - Giglio, Louie. *I am not but I know I AM*. Sisters, OR. Multnomah Publishers Inc., 2005.

16 - Bentorah, Chaim. *Hebrew Word Study: A Hebrew Teacher's Call to Silence*. Parker, CO. Outskirts Press Inc., 2013.

17 - *St. Stephen's Society*. 1/F Great Wall Factory Building, 11 Cheung Shun Street, Cheung Sha Wan, Hong Kong. info@ststephenssociety.com

18 - *Green Pastures*. Registered Office: 9 Mornington Road, Southport, Merseyside, PR9 0TS.

19 - Lewis, C S. *Mere Christianity (revised edition)*. San Francisco, CA. Harper San Francisco, 2009.

20 - Bentorah, Chaim. *Hebrew Word Study: A Hebrew Teacher Explores the Heart of God*. Bloomington, IN. WestBow Press, 2013.

21 - Wiester, John L. *The Genesis Connection*. Hatfield, PA. Interdisciplinary Biblical Research Institute, 1983.

Printed in the United States
By Bookmasters